BENEDICT'S POOL

Also available in this series:

BENEDICT'S POOL

Fred Archer

ISIS
LARGE PRINT
Oxford and Orlando

First published in Great Britain 1999
by Sutton Publishing Limited

Published in Large Print 2000 by ISIS Publishing Ltd,
7 Centremead, Osney Mead, Oxford OX2 0ES, and
ISIS Publishing, PO Box 195758,
Winter Springs, Florida 32719-5758, USA
by arrangement with Sutton Publishing Limited

British Library Cataloguing in Publication Data
Archer, Fred, 1915–99
  Benedict's Pool. – Large print ed.
  1. Country life – England – Worcestershire – Anecdotes
  2. Haunted places – England – Worcestershire – Anecdotes
  3. Large type books
  I. Title
  942.4'4'0823

ISBN 0-7531-5793-4 (hb)
ISBN 0-7531-5794-2 (pb)

Printed and bound by Antony Rowe, Chippenham and Reading

CONTENTS

INTRODUCTION

Behind the Monastery at the foot of Bredon Hill, close by the village of Netherstone and enclosed by two coppices, there lies Benedict's Pool. This watery dell is not so much a landmark — although it is more than well known by all who live nearby — as a spooky dent in the limestone. Here the moorhens nest on the little island where the foxtails grow and the king cups show that vivid yellow by the water's edge. It is true that the Pool holds some coarse fish, tench, roach and lots of eels, but few villagers will fish for them in the waters beneath those dark coppices where the sun seldom peeps through the trees. Joe Green, custodian of Parson's Folly, the low tower on Bredon's summit, was indeed a man and a half, afraid of no one, but not even Joe would go near Benedict's Pool on moonlit nights.

Writing of the villagers of Netherstone in the 1920s brings back vivid memories of a time gone by — of corduroys, hobnails, Oxford shirts, mufflers, cider drinking and twist-tobacco chewing men of such great character. In this book we are privileged to meet the folk who lived near Benedict's Pool, whose lives were governed by the ways of the land and the turning of the seasons. The Bullen brothers of Cobblers Quar, Alf the shepherd and James the carter, set the scene. They worked the land for Tom Samson when shire horses with their ploughs skimmed the shallow limestone hill, and that thin Cotswold soil was fertilised by the great Cotswold sheep — wedders and tegs in the pens of hurdled turnips — and not by the chemical mixtures used today.

I wonder how Alfred trimmed, or belted, the stained wool off his ewes, and whether he made liquid manure in a cider barrel with the beltings. And James, when he mowed the sainfoin clover (called the holy hay), he had no need of a cultivated flower garden; the pink blooms of that clover, the fodder for the livestock, were his garden.

Here, too, we find the likes of Jarvie Ricketts, ex-gamekeeper and a great storyteller, and his tight-lipped wife Ada, and Jack Lampit and Queenie White, the one he lived along with, as folks described such a relationship, who had been a lady until drink rather changed things. And we must not forget the Revd George Mellor, who went astray with his maid Hannah Loosestrife, and Sep Sands, the poacher and ne'er-do-well who spent his time at the old Cider Mill. That little bit of Gloucestershire, where Worcestershire comes in alongside in the Butts, teems with folks such as these.

My writing describes this part of the Hill from early in the century until the Great War, a time when life was not easy for these men and their families, working a six-day week and living in thatched, half-timbered cottages that could be cold and damp with no central heating, running water, or even indoor bathrooms like today. No one should romanticise life in those early years, when the ploughman of the Hill thought nothing of walking eleven miles to plough a single acre. No, life was hard then.

Even so, one thing is certain — the labourer and his family were always content with their lot. At the end of the day, as the tea-time fire in their cottages gave warmth to their bodies, they had time to think and they dwelt on the wonders of the world around them. The rusty plough share shining again on the headland, the crab apples and berries in the hedgerow, the lambs in the blossom of the orchard. Life was not easy, but it had its compensations for these simple countryfolk who lived off the land and knew its ways so well.

This book is full of the folklore, traditions and customs of a people who were steeped in superstition and leavened by religion. But we must not condemn the villagers their interest in the unexplained in that pre-wireless age, for surely we are all curious about the mysteries of life. But the villagers also adhered to the principles of the Church, and these two elements — their folklore and their faith — went side by side for these rural folk and formed the foundation on which they built their lives.

I look at this story as an opera staged on the Hill, where each character has an opinion to voice, a role to play and a contribution to bring to a life that was precious. I wonder if it might cause us to question whether life today is so much improved after all.

CHAPTER ONE

Ploughman and Shepherd

On a bleak March morning in 1902 on the flat of Bredon Hill the gale on this limestone outcrop of the Cotswolds was doubling a group of firs in the spinney like bent ploughmen. Here, near the Parish quarry, the old badger setts honeycombed the land of elder and hawthorn. The wiry grass of the Hill rippled in waves like an incoming tide. Down below, in a little coppice, the tall poplar trees squealed as they rubbed shoulders with their neighbours — the locals described it as an unkid sound — unkind and eerie. The only green on these trees was the mistletoe high up swinging in the gale, a parasite which had grown on Bredon since the time of the Druids. It favoured oaks, apple and hawthorn as well as the poplar.

The Druids of ancient times had cut the mistletoe from the oak as they worshipped the Sun God. The mystic plant was cut with a golden sickle, falling into a white cloth worked with gold, and then a very solemn religious procession would make its way to a semicircular bank on the Hill where the King and Queen Stones stood side by side, lifelike with their semblance of human heads. These Druid folk maintained that the stones had fallen

1

from Heaven and were known as Mercury and Minerva, the patrons of wisdom.

The men working on the Hill that day in March were conscious of how their ancestors had lived. Alfred Bullen, the shepherd, could neither read nor write yet he was knowledgeable about some of the history and folklore of the Hill. The young men of the Hill farms reckoned the Hill to be an unkid place of evil spirits, but their fathers had a respect for its antiquity. Stories handed down from father to son, the oral tradition, gave Alfred much food for thought. He knew where the Horse Camps were, an amphitheatre twenty-five yards in diameter excavated on Furze Hill. It was here the men of the Hill had kept their horses and cattle at night, safe from the wolves that roamed this lonely spot in olden times. The Roman Saltway lay below. Field names still smacked of the Roman occupation.

Young men have visions, old men have dreams; this 64-year-old shepherd had both. Alfred looked upon the King and Queen Stones with a kind of reverence and regularly attended the Court held there at Easter when the stones were whitewashed. Delicate children, especially those suffering from rickets, were taken there and pushed between those life-sized rocks while an Officer of the Court said the words, "May the Spirit of the Hills be with you." Alfred was loath to admit that as a youngster with rickets he was put between the stones and now, at sixty-four years of age, he was still attending the Court Leet.

On this March morning on the Hill Alfred's brother James, four years younger than the shepherd, was walking the furrow behind his team of horses ploughing the field where Alfred had almost finished hitching, or folding, his flock of yearling sheep known as tegs and wethers, on turnips.

The bachelor brothers lived together in a stone cottage known as Cobblers Quar. Life at Cobblers Quar was not always harmonious! James had learned to read and write, which somewhat riled Alfred. With Alfred Bullen, a lifelong shepherd, and James Bullen, a carter/ploughman, a kind of Cain and Abel relationship existed. The dialect of the men was essentially Gloucestershire but it smacked sometimes of Shakespeare — Stratford, the home of the Bard, was but twenty miles away.

Tom Samson, their employer who had returned from the Boer War, had sort of "inherited" the brothers from his father's farm. Tom had served in the County Yeomanry. He was a stocky chap, who had just celebrated his fifty-sixth birthday. Handsome in a rural sense with dark auburn hair, greying at the edges, under a grey bowler hat, he was a superb horseman. While this up-and-coming farmer had inherited the two older men to work the land, the horse team can only be described as "long in the tooth". James's two-horse team ploughing the few inches of soil above the limestone on Bredon were Colonel and Captain. They worked abreast pulling a single-furrow plough. Alfred, watching his brother ploughing, listened to the age-old commands: "Cup, Colonel. Ett, Captain. Ett furrow I said! Damn your pelt you wasted life, think I stole ya?" (Ett was a command for a horse to go to the right.)

3

Leaning on a hurdle smoking his pipe, Alfred called to his brother. "How bist a getting on with the ploughing, you? Why doesn't set the furrow wheel a bit light and make a tidy job turning over the mould?"

This chivelling was usual between the brothers and, as James turned his team on the headland, he replied, "A smartish fellow thee bist telling me how to set the plough, thee a squat on a hurdle, never going above a chain from thee farting ship. As't got the kettle on the boil on the brash fire under the wall?"

Alfred ignored his brother's comments, replying, "See how the fir trees bend their yuds in this March wind and the college birds [Jackdaws] be in the burra of the Quar. 'Tis only a cat lap I be brewing on the fire, you have emptied our costrels of cider happen."

James's response was as usual. "Ay the costrel barrel's empty. I sat under the pollard oaks halfway up the hill by the spring and finished the cider. I've filled the barrel with water from the spring, but mind ya, the cider puts heart into a chap."

Alfred meanwhile sat on a heap of stones under the wall and poured tea from an iron kettle into two enamel mugs. Despite the friction that existed between these brothers of the Hill farm the same ritual took place at bait time when the plough followed the folded sheep. The sheep had a fresh pen of roots every day folded by hurdles and James tried to keep up with his plough on the cleared land. This land would be planted with barley in April, fertilised by the sheep.

The men stood by the remnants of the fire with their thumb pieces of bread and cheese. Alfred took the cottage loaf from his frail basket and divided the cheese. He then poured out two more cups of tea into the enamel cups. As James's horses stood waiting in the furrow with their backs to the howling wind Alfred teased his brother, saying, "Dost reckon them two dunnels of shine ull run away with the plough while we has our bait under the wall?"

James, not too proud of his team, answered, "What! Captain and Colonel? Gunpowder udn't shift them two craters! It's time past that our Gaffer, Tom Salmon, sent them to the knackers and bought me some tolerable horse flesh."

Alfred thought for a moment, then said, "That reminds me, our Gaffer wants me to cut the young lambs tomorrow. That's if the wind drops."

As Alfred glanced up at the sky, a skud of rain came over the firs and behind that a blue sky made a picture of the Severn Vale, and Gloucester Cathedral glistened gold some twenty miles away.

"That's as maybe," the ploughman replied, "and it's no concern of mine."

"Well it is, James," Alfred quickly responded, "because it's thy job to hold the lambs while I castrate them and cut their tails." Alfred's flock of Cotswold ewes and lambs was in the big orchard below the Cuckoo Pen and the lambs were hearty and strong.

Next morning proved dry and sunny with a soft wind from the south-west. No respectable stockman would cut the lambs in an east wind. Alfred's dog Rosie had penned the ewes and lambs in the Old Cross Barn, a thatched piece of history where Roman numerals marked the joints of the huge elm trusses in the roof under the thatch.

Tom Samson, the young farmer, arrived from his farmhouse just below the Cuckoo Pen. He was riding a chestnut, weight-carrying hunter; he needed such a gelding being a man of fifteen stone.

"Morning men," he announced as he entered through the front door of the barn, doors built to take a loaded wagon of hay or corn. He shut the big blacksmith-made asp behind him and viewed his flock, which occupied about three-quarters of the barn floor. The other quarter, where the cutting was to be done, was strewn with straw to accommodate the lambs after their operation.

"Morning Gaffer," Alfred replied. "'Tis a nice March morning. I see the rooks be busy over in the coppice. Have you brought the twist bacca Sir?"

"Oh, yes Alfred. Here's a four-ounce packet, enough for your pipe after the castration."

As James caught the first lamb, a ram lamb, he held it by its four legs against his chest. Alfred was already chewing the twist tobacco and held a bone-handled shut knife in his hand, a knife that had been used by his father Old Aaran Bullen.

Deftly Alfred cut off a part of the lamb's purse, squeezed it until two testicles emerged. With his teeth he grabbed the testicles, pulled back until the cord broke, then he spat the sweetbreads, as they are called, into a bucket. He then spat some of the juice of the twist tobacco into the wound. James put the lamb onto its feet again and Alfred cut off its tail. This went on all day. The ewe lambs were lucky but they did bleed more than the ram lambs. Alfred was keeping some of the best of the ewe lambs for breeding when they were two years old. James noticed that his brother left the tails of these young potential breeding sheep a bit longer.

As Tom Samson caught the lambs to bring them to James he smiled when the carter, quick to criticise his brother, said, "Ay, Brother, what's the idea you be leaving longer tails on some of the young yow lambs. Bist losing thee grip?"

Tom Samson knew why the tails were left longer as Alfred explained. "When you sit a ewe up to trim its feet or dress it for maggots or give it a drench, it sits more comfortable with a tail to sit on," as he said, "rather than a bare ass."

It was a gorey scene in the barn. Alfred's whiskered face was crimson with blood. Whether the twist tobacco acted as a disinfectant after the operation is debatable but it certainly saved the shepherd from the taste of blood. The twist was strong; the remainder would fuel his clay pipe.

It was mid-afternoon when the flock returned to the orchard, the lambs glad to rejoin their mothers where the ewes' milk compensated a little for their suffering. Alfred's father and grandfather had performed the same operation back in the last century. It was very rare to lose a lamb.

Next morning Alfred made the last hurdled pen on the turnip field. He would move his flock of wethers and teas the next day ready for the spring sale. James still had a little of the field to plough. The wind had dropped and the peewits were doing their fancy flights overhead, a reconnaissance to find the best place to lay their eggs in the adjoining field. Larks soared into the blue sky, and nature gave a hint of spring. Soon the Hill would be alive with the song of nesting birds. It was one of those quiet mornings on the Hill. Alfred and James sat having their bait, resting their tired legs, a sort of mid-morning siesta. Suddenly James gave a cry and Rosie, Alfred's sheepdog, pricked her ears.

"Hark!" the carter said, "there's rumbling under my homucks. Dost reckon it's badgers under my feet?" James lay down with his ear close to the ground and Rosie pawed the soil under the wall.

Alfred, still eating his bread and cheese, exclaimed, "There's evil spirits on this hill. I hear the sound of men marching. Lors a mercy, the earth moves!" The wall on the edge of the stone quarry was close to where Tom Samson's men had recently taken away some stone to repair the village lane. Now the face of the quarry crumbled, bringing a heap of stones to the quarry floor with a noise like a peal of thunder.

"Thee bist trying to put the breeze up me Alfred, talking of evil spirits and marching men when 'twas only a fall of stones in the quarry." James's voice was full of relief.

"Well," Alfred replied in no more than a whisper, "thurs things on this hill as be far from being natural. I'm no scholard but they do say that an underground passage runs under the Hill from the old Monastery to Benedict's Pool, then on to the Castle. I'll ask David Hicks the gamekeeper when he comes up here. David's about this hill all times of day and night around his traps and wires. He will tell if anything unnatural takes place."

As James walked gingerly to his waiting horses, making sparks with his hobnailed boots over the stones, Alfred just stood and stared as if in a trance. This was too much for his brother, who called out, "Bist a gwain to move thee ship into the last pen on the turnips or stand and gawp at me all day? I have got to finish the ploughing this week ready for the barley planting at Easter."

Alfred, still standing by the wall, then called for James to return to the dying fire. "Can you spare a minute, your horses won't move. I've a question to ask you." He knew that his brother hadn't slept the night before, and now was the time to ask why. "What's on your mind, Brother?"

James was loathe to respond but finally told his tale. "I don't rightly like to tell ya but it's what happened when I went down the Hill with the horses at knocking off time at the edge of night. The full moon had just rose over the Cotswolds and I was stopping at the Cuckoo Pen to drink that beautiful water from the spring there. You understand, I always fills my costrel and a quart bottle to take home, the water's so clear. I stooped down with my enamel cup to get a drink and my eyes damn near popped out of my head. The water was purple, almost crimson in the moonlight as it gushed out under the beech trees. You know the Parson told us that when the end of the world comes the moon will turn to blood. When I saw that purple water my feet hardly touched the ground. My two horses had a job to keep up with me past Paris and Camp House. They knew their way to the stable but I was frit to death on that hill. I don't think the

9

Almighty is very pleased with us on this hill ever since we made such a noise with the church bells at the New Year. Parson said 'twas desecration and I was mixed up in it."

Then Alfred explained, "Joe Baker the water diviner was trying to prove his point that the water on Spring Hill that went underground was the same source as that at the Cuckoo Pen. A better supply was wanted for the villages. Joe and the Churchwardens put permanganate of Potash in the water on Spring Hill and were about to walk to the Cuckoo Pen to see the purple coloured water when they saw you hurry down the Hill going hell for leather.

"Well, James, I've only heard rumours of what happened New Year's morning but you be one of the bell-ringers and you have kept it quiet. Get on with a few more furrows and I'll finish the pen. The peewits make a charm as they circle up above, and the twittering of the larks be company for a man alone with his sheep."

Alfred stood a while and watched the peewits follow his brother's plough, picking up every worm. Later, as they sat by their log fire after having a meal of boiled fat bacon, potatoes and turnips, the older brother came to a decision. "James, it's about time you told me the truth about what happened in St Lawrence's Church early on New Year's Day."

James was a bit hesitant. He didn't want to let down the Captain of the Tower, who was actually responsible for the scene that New Year's morning. Old Frank was a sensible man when he called out the rotation for the bell-ringers to change ringing. He had inherited from his grandfather the art of ringing the changes or just the simple one, two, three, four, five in certain orders.

New Year's Eve in 1901 had not been Frank's night. Oh, the bells rang merrily from ten o'clock, ringing until the vital hour. The Old Year was dying and, when the last hour before its death at midnight came, the bells of St Lawrence always rang a half muffled peal, a peal otherwise only rung at funerals.

James began, "You know Frank when he's had too much to drink. Tom Samson, who had newly been made the Churchwarden, took a whole lot of rum to the ringers in the tower. It was a cold night and Frank's thoughts were for the ringers. Well, you know, Alfred, I'm a moderate cider drinker, I had a tot or two of the rum. God knows how much Frank drank."

"What happened then, James?" Alfred knew things had gone wrong but didn't know why. James sat back from the fire and mopped his brow. "Thee bist asweating smartish, Brother, sure you're alright?"

"It all comes back like a dream, Alfred, a bad dream. I can see it now. Old Frank climbing up to the bells with the leather mufflers. You see, the leathers on the one side muffle the sound of the bells. Some calls it a buff peal. He fumbled up there for I don't know how long, but midnight had past, the old year had gone without the usual ritual. Oh, it was half past one in the morning when we rang a kind of half-muffled peal all out of step. A hell of a rattle. Folks left their beds, opened windows and wondered. By half past two we gave it best and finished the rum that the Churchwarden had given us.

"There was almost a calamity when we did ring.

Young Sam Close was pulling the rope and his tie got caught, lifting him up to the ceiling of the ringing chamber. What a night! But as the bells stood at rest with the clappers or mufflers still left where Frank had fixed them five men, including me, slept in the bell chamber. There was Holy Communion arranged for eight o'clock the following morning and we were snoring away and the Vicar arrived. Desecrating a Holy Place, Revd Cuthbert told us, and that no doubt the Almighty would have his revenge. It has bin a strange spring, Brother, very strange, and it's said even the Revd Vernon has been going off the rails."

Men of the village at the turn of the century were steeped in religion. The Parson spoke of such things as Apostolic succession, Transubstantiation (the Body and Blood of Christ being present in the Bread and Wine), of the Virgin Birth and other great spiritual topics. The knowledge of the vengeance of the Almighty and of the power of the Devil had two effects on the brothers and their neighbours. On the one hand, it scared them into living honest, upright lives, but on the other, there was comfort in the thought that someone above was looking after you and, of course, life everlasting was a foregone conclusion. This emphasis on the spiritual side of life gave men like the ploughman and the shepherd something of a staddle — like the framework supporting a corn rick.

But the religion of the Church was mixed with the people's own ancient ancestral stories, and so they lived in a kind of limbo, midway between the two. The folklore warned not to burn elder wood on the fire, but it was so that the Devil — not some evil folklore spirit — would not come down the chimney. The people remained fearful of both. Any change in the local scene upset the old ancestral ways and rhythms of life, but it was to the conventional Church that the people turned. The Revd Cuthbert, the Vicar of Netherstone, had a stabilising influence on their lives; he guided the men of Netherstone and they relied on him.

The Vicar was careful not to disregard the views and ancient stories of the villagers. Indeed, he had a bent for local history and held meetings at the Vicarage. Alfred vividly recalled the stories of the Iron Age Camp on the summit of Bredon Hill. Here, near the tower built by Squire Parsons in 1795, are relics of times on the Hill before Christ. Revd Cuthbert spoke of the camp of 220 acres surrounded by a ditch, and of a tribe of Belgae invading Britain in the first century BC. They were the last invaders before the Roman occupation. Fearsome fighters, these Belgae, but also up-to- date farmers of the time, who constructed a level to cultivate the valley of the Avon. Cuthbert described how the Hill Folk came to a sad end at the hand of these invaders. The Belgae gave no quarter to the Hill Folk, and a bloody battle resulted in the annihilation of the native men. Mutilated skeletons were discovered. The Banbury Stone near the camp stood alone, dedicated to the Sun God, a relic of Celtic superstition.

The people on the Hill did rely on the Parson, it is true, but other factors also held sway in the lives of these good countryfolk. The branch railway that ran in the Vale below set a timetable for work and rest. Watches were set by the little tank engine's smoke wafting through the withy trees of the Carrant Brook valley below. Alfred and James saw pictures in the fire as their logs burned on winter nights and the sparks made orange and blue patterns at the chimney bottom. "A frost!" they would chant together as these things were noticed. The tawny owl calling in the woods gave the men an accurate forecast of the next day's fine weather. There was no end to the ways in which nature told the labourers what was in store: crows at break-necks was a sign of rain to come; bree flies, the bloodsuckers that plagued James's horses, warned of whirlwinds. All these things had been proved long before the Christian religion came to Bredon, things which Alfred and James took for granted but never fully understood.

But what would life be without its mysteries when all is explained and tidy. Men worked hard in the fields all day accompanied by the music of the birds, the rustling of trees. They had their memories, their thoughts of time and eternity. They understood how some things in nature worked with them, and how others were a threat. When the badgers scooped out the wasp nests on the Hill to make a meal of the grubs and turned the cow's turds in the meadow for the insects underneath, nature was simply keeping a balance.

CHAPTER
TWO

The Horse Camps and
The Amphitheatre

Tom Samson's daughter Ruth, now seventeen, had told the Bullens a little of the Roman occupation of the Hill. She was a bright girl and had a good education — quite unusual for a girl so early in the century — and she had a keen interest in the history of the local area. She explained how the Horse Camps on Furze Hill had been constructed to protect the Roman's horses from the ravaging wolves at night time. The Amphitheatre on the Hill was a stopping place for the Romans with their panniers loaded with salt on their way from Droitwich to the coast. Often the men had passed this furze hollow on their way to the Cider Mill pub.

As Easter came in 1902 Tom Samson sold his yearling sheep at the Evesholm Market. Alfred brought his ewes and lambs to the hill pastures. James had planted the barley on the Turnip field. On Good Friday, of all days, the brothers planted their early potatoes in the garden at Cobblers Quar. As they walked across the Hill to collect firewood from the firs they noticed what they thought were early mushrooms growing in the coppice.

"They looks alright, Brother. We will have them along with some home cured bacon at tea time."

The hooped pan swung on the pot hooks above the flames and the fat of the bacon turned the mushrooms a deep pink colour. The smell of the cooking was unusual, "perfumes of the east" Alfred called it. He cut the loaf, dipped a thick slice in the fat and said, "Moreish, Brother."

When the meal was over Alfred and James took a walk, lantern in hand, towards the Cider Mill passing the Horse Camps on their way. David Hicks was along the footpath looking around a few rabbit snares he had set by the badger setts. By the light of his lantern he looked on the two men, who appeared to be half-drunk. They swayed and they stumbled along the footpath. David wished them "Good Night."

Alfred replied, "See you shortly in the Cider Mill."

The moon rose over the Cotswold Edge, but that was a usual sight. Over the Horse Camps Alfred called out, "Thurs a light over that Roman place, a bright light over the Horse Camps."

James held his brother's arm, shouting, "Lord I be frit amus to death. I can see the Roman soldiers sat in a circle around the holla."

In their emotional state — aided by the "magic" mushrooms — they saw a dangerous army. The men saw in the Amphitheatre a number of horses resting with their packs of salt, more salt stacked near by and, in the enclosure behind the fence, a small flock of sheep safe from the wolves, chewing their cud under the moon, sheep that would be slaughtered to feed the soldiers on their way to the south coast.

Soldiers stood around the fire cooking a meal. Tomorrow they would head for the Fosseway, the Saltway, with their loads, towards the coast of Devon, then over the sea to Gaul.

James stood behind Alfred and whispered, "Who's that on the throne?"

At that moment, Emperor Claudius called out, "As I sit on this throne of gold, this throne of judgement on Starn Hill, the Pavement, take heed men of Netherstone to my commands. Do you read the Word of God? Who's your Priest?"

As he spoke, a rumble of thunder followed some lightning. "Hasten over the badger setts," Alfred gasped as he grabbed James by the arm pleading with him to take a short cut to Cobblers Quar. "We are not going to the Cider Mill tonight!" he said softly, and quietly the brothers left the Horse Camp shaded from the full moon by a line of beech trees.

Cobblers Quar was like an oasis in a desert. Alfred put another log on the dwindling fire and, when the big iron kettle boiled, James made two mugs of cocoa. They both nodded off in the firelight and the oil lamp swung from a beam, cold and unlit. Every few minutes one brother would wake with a start, usually James, who whispered, careful not to be overheard by any spirits or Roman soldiers, "Bist all right, Alfred? Shall us go to bed?"

And so to bed they went. Their dreams were as if true until morning broke with understandable relief.

* * *

Next morning Alfred was making a pen for his ewes and lambs on a field of kale a little way from the turnip field, a strong walled-in enclosure known as Fiddlers Knap. The iron crowbar weighed heavy on the old man's arms as he drove in the ash stakes which he then tied to withy hurdles. The yearling sheep had gone to market, and his ewes and lambs relished the green of the rape after the lambing in the Vale where the only green thing they found was the ivy at the hedge bottom during that dry cold spring when the grass was loathe to grow.

James had planted the barley and his two horses pulled a set of zigzag harrows covering the seed. The geldings were aged but James, now sixty years old, wondered how he would cope with the nimble young horses that Tom Samson had promised to replace the team.

Alfred left his flock when he saw the smoke of the ten o'clock train leave Netherstone station, walking from Fiddlers Knap, his route took him past the Dew Pond, partly hidden by a clump of beech trees. Whether the Dew Pond functioned or not, was it a part of the folklore of the Hill? Tom Samson did as his father before him to provide water for his ewe stock in summer. As the snow filled the gully on Spring Hill, six or seven feet deep most winters, Alfred and James loaded carts of the white stuff and made a type of rick over the Dew Pond. With several hundred gallons of water from the melted snow, it was a godsend for Tom Samson in dry summers on the Hill.

As the men had their bait under the wall Tom Samson arrived on his weight-carrying hunter. He had ridden across the Hill from Shaldon. His farmhouse there, a stone-built house capped with Cotswold tiles, stood alongside his barn and stables with the cattle shed, all sheltered by a row of fir trees.

"Morning Gaffer," James spoke as he sat on a corn sack under the wall. "My horses don't sweat so much today, the harrows be light but they be so nation slow when hitched to the plough."

"I know Captain and Colonel have got long in the tooth, and now Alfred's wethers are gone to market I'll buy you two three-year-olds at Barton Fair."

James stood up beside his horses, patting them on their rounded backs, and sighed, "You two boys have been good servants to me and the Gaffer, but now I got summat to look forward to, to be sure."

Tom Samson accompanied Alfred back to Fiddlers Knap. When they arrived he tied his horse up to a hawthorn bush and, with Alfred, sized up his flock. Some of the early lambs were looking what they called "kind".

"Don't spare the cake and the oats, Alfred. We might have a few of the best of the lambs fat for Whitsun."

Alfred then continued with his crowbar, carrying four hurdles on his back to make another pen for the next day. Tom Samson looked with satisfaction at his flock and at the aged shepherd, a man who had folded sheep on Bredon for his father. "By the way, Alfred, David Hicks, my gamekeeper, was worried about you and your brother last night. He expected you at the Cider Mill but said you turned back at the Horse Camps."

"Oh, Master Samson, I'd like to forget the incident last night under that full moon. The Devil was loose I'm sure. What we saw was real, Gaffer. A man on a throne. But we've done nothing wrong — it appears we have to suffer for the sins of others."

As Tom Samson went home for his tea the 5.20 train steamed out of Netherstone station. James took his horses from the turnip field to the stable at Shaldon. Peewits were calling plaintively overhead; they would soon be nesting. As Alfred made his way to Cobblers Quar he looked down over Netherstone where, in the field below, two hares were boxing quite oblivious of Alfred and his dog Rosie. He thought that phrase "As mad as a March hare" just summed up their experiences last night at the Horse Camps.

Before we condemn Alfred and James Bullen for what may be called hallucinations from eating the magic mushrooms, let us remember that Bredon Hill is steeped in history.

The Roman coins turned up by the plough, the Samaen-ware pottery alongside Battery Wood, are but some of the ancient relics of by-gone days that have been unearthed. When James Bullen scratched the surface of the limestone hill with his plough and Alfred fattened his sheep, the Cotswold breed almost as high as the hurdles, the Hill still jealously guarded its secrets. The morning mists still capped the summit when a bright summer day followed. The legend that these mists filled the ancient Dew Pond had been believed. The Roman sentry no doubt shivered on that windswept hill, longing for the warm Italian plains The old trenches near the Banbury Stone were softened by time and the springing turf.

Ancient barns stood in the Bullens' time, a reminder of their ancestral origins, but it was the trees that seemed eternal, for beech may stand sentinel for hundreds of years. The beech trees on Bredon stood as if troubled by the distant past, and, indeed, spirits of the ancient soldiers were said to live on in those beeches, Briton, Roman, and Saxon. There was an influence deep down below the turf that fed their roots. Wars, feuds, quarrels, events and men of long ago are never forgotten by those trees: men who, as drovers, wandered with their flocks on Bredon, who watched the fogs on Longdon Marsh and who listened at night to the bark of the wolves; ancient Britons who prowled cautiously around the Roman camps, an earlier savage race who seem to have been allied more to the stunted, twisted hawthorn than to the great beeches who stand sentinel, their roots deep, touching the graves of these fighting men. Men and sheep sleep but not the trees; they have longer memories of wars when the Hill was but a moor of golden gorse and great boare thistles.

CHAPTER
THREE

At the Cider Mill

After Tom Samson had checked with his two men, Alfred made straight for Cobblers Quar to prepare the evening meal. James had his horses to feed and water at Shaldon. The fire in the open hearth still smouldered from morning; it soon livened up when an armful of dry gorse was added, sending the flames up the chimney. Alfred slung the iron kettle on the pot hooks that hung from a sway in the chimney. He then put a couple of eggs in a saucepan of water at the edge of the fire. The wind still blew like a March wind although it was now early April. Going to the shed for more wood, Alfred thought of his father's saying: "March doesn't finish until the 12th of April". That was so true. Before the calender was changed about 1755, March did end on what is now 12 April.

James arrived at six o'clock. He put his frail basket on a shelf alongside the fireplace and had his meal with Alfred on a scrubbed deal table. Bread and butter, a boiled egg and a lump of bread pudding made the previous day. James's horses were pulling the clover from their racks in the stable. He would walk back and turn them out onto the Hill after tea.

It was seven before the meal was finished. The brothers sat a while staring at the fire, as the oil lamp swung on a chain over the table. While James returned to see to his horses Alfred washed the crocks in the old brown sink. Then he took a bucket from underneath it, lit a hurricane lamp and went to the well in the garden, pumping water ready for the following day.

The wind blew strong and made eerie noises in the firs by the stable. James had ladled water from the Dew Pond to the stone trough nearby. Colonel and Captain drank, and James thought to himself, "I could do with a drink after what's happened lately." He returned to Cobblers Quar cottage with a little candle lantern.

Alfred had his top coat on ready for a walk over the Hill to the Cider Mill. The two brothers walked silently along the footpath near the badger earths by the light of the candle lantern. "'Tis a pity there's no Parish Lantern tonight, Alfred. The clouds cover the moon."

Alfred replied, "It's the middle of the week and we don't often go drinking until the week-end, but we can do with a livener."

As rabbits scurried around in all directions another light shone from across the Hill. David Hicks was going the rounds of his wire snares, picking up the milky does and the strong bucks. They don't make good eating but the keeper would find a market for them somewhere.

The lights of the Cider Mill shone across the orchard of Joe Badger, the Landlord, welcoming the men from Cobblers Quar. Down in Netherstone lights shone out too from that mixture of thatch and Cotswold stone.

23

The Cider Mill itself was a thatched inn built in half-timber, black and white, a feature of the long building, the timbers forming rough squares of tarred wood, the panels a creamy white. Inside the front door stood a crock-faced grandfather clock bought by Joe's father on his wedding day. Joe Badger kept a good fire going in the dog grate, and Alfred and James felt at home as they sat together on a curved settle in the inglenook.

When Joe mentioned that the wind was cold for April this brought the usual retort from James, "'Tis that skinny wind from Russia; there's no shelter from it between yer and the Ural Mountains, so the Parson says." With that he took the poker and thrust it in the flames of the wood fire. "There!" he said to Alfred, "that poker when it's red hot is going in my cider. It's called a mulled drink."

Sep Sands spent a lot of his time at the Cider Mill, apart from when he was poaching rabbits. He had been idly by the fire all day but had netted a few rabbits the night before. "My season's almost over," he boasted as he held a pewter mug full of best beer.

"That's what education does for you," Alfred whispered to his brother. "Breeds idleness."

Sep Sands was what is politely called a "love child", being the son of Widow Sands fathered by Tom Samson when he was but nineteen. It happened one hay-making time when Tom's father's cows, worried by the bree fly, took off over the Hill to Sunshine Farm, where Widow Sands kept a few cows and sheep. Widow Sands' husband had died soon after their marriage, but she soldiered on with those forty acres. She made a living

24

making butter and selling it in a local shop and feeding pigs with the skim milk and barley meal. When Tom Samson went to fetch the cows from Sunshine Farm, the young widow helped to part the animals from her small herd of Shorthorns.

With Samson's cows safely back at Shaldon, Widow Sands invited Tom back to Sunshine Farm for a drink of her homemade wine. Was it beetroot or elderberry? Tom never remembered, but he and Widow Sands — a dark attractive woman of twenty-eight — sat out in the garden that summer evening mellowed by the wine, tired after a day in the hay field, until twilight fell and the owl hooted "Tu-whit, tu-whoo" over the fir trees. Tom had a feeling for that dark-haired woman that he had never quite felt before.

Finally, Daisy said, "I must shut up the fowl before the fox is around. Just come and see my young cockerels." The young country couple leant together on the five-barred gate by the fowl pen, and instinctively their arms enfolded and their lips met in the twilight. Together they walked through the gate where the small hay field had scented hay fit to carry. Daisy's brother was coming up the next day with his wagon to help her rick the fodder, and the hay was in little cocks ready for carrying.

As Tom Samson sat beside the attractive widow he felt so much a part of a natural instinct, a feeling that men and maids had experienced since time began. They lay as much intoxicated by the scent of the hay as by the wine they had drunk. Soon they made love. Tom felt a satisfaction he had never had before, and Daisy admitted she loved him.

Sep Sands was the result of that evening at Sunshine Farm. Tom supported his lover — she lacked nothing all her widowed life — but Sep was not the comfort to her she deserved. He was work shy, and spent too much time at the Cider Mill. Eventually, Tom Samson married a farmer's daughter from off the Cotswolds, a lady who joined him hunting with the foxhounds around Bredon. They had one child, a daughter, Ruth.

Back at the Cider Mill, stories from the brothers Bullen of tunnels that honeycombed the Hill and of evil spirits made Sep Sands sit open-mouthed, as he half believed the old men. Joe Badger had been talking at the week-end to Tom and Sarah Samson's daughter Ruth. She had studied geology and had told Joe that the limestone ridge, a part of the Cotswolds of which Bredon is an offshoot, stretched from Lincolnshire in the north to West Dorset in the south. She had spoken of the landslip near Parson's Folly, the Banbury Stone and of the lady riding her horse and her narrow escape when the land went from under the horse's feet. She had recounted the tale about the small granary of wheat, which had been stored underground for centuries, being exposed, and how, at about this time, a large landslide had occurred in West Dorset.

Joe the Hermit, who lived in a barn near the Folly and was custodian of that tower, could spin a fine tale and joined in the fireside storytelling. He had been at the barn feeding the pig he called Jesus when a crack occurred in the limestone between the tower and the barn. The whole Iron Age camp seemed to move three feet down the Hill causing a rumble like thunder. Sep Sands, although a devious character, listened in astonishment, but believed Ruth's tales because they had been written in one of her books. David Hicks reckoned that the Hill was one great graveyard. He dug up a skeleton human skull near the Horse Camp with teeth like ivory

Alfred asked, "What, over by the General's Brake? I'll go to Hell if I haven't come over in a muck sweat."

Joe Badger retorted, "Sit back from the fire then. This hawthorn wood gives some heat, and that'll make you sweat."

James drank the last dregs of cider from the crock pot, saying, "Them as lives longest sees the most."

But the brothers had been fortified by Joe Badger's cider and took the footpath over the Hill, with lantern lit, towards Cobblers Quar. It did mean skirting the coppice by Benedict's Pool, what James would call an unkid place. As they left, the grandfather clock warned for the hour of ten. The brothers heard the strike as they went through Joe's orchard. Along the footpath the men were not alone but were not afraid of the usual things on that April night, the squealing of a vixen, the hooting of owls and the whistling of plovers, the grunting of badgers and the coughing and farting of the sheep. They had a certain faith and reliance on God but knew that sometimes the Devil, Beelzebub himself, had sway on the Hill.

It was a strange sight as the brothers made their way to Cobblers Quar, James holding the candle lantern, Alfred walking with his shepherd's crook in one hand

and the other hand hooked in James's arm. The lantern illuminated the footpath but the shadows cast were dark and foreboding.

On clear nights, when a multitude of stars covered the sky, Alfred would remind his brother of the Pole Star and how their father called the stars around that star "Jack and his Wagon"; it was normally called The Plough. They marvelled at shooting stars. Life was full of mystery on the Hill.

CHAPTER
FOUR

The Bald-headed Woman in the Moonlight

Jarvie Ricketts, gamekeeper on Alstone, an estate belonging to Netherstone situated on the western slopes of Bredon Hill, was a wiry little man who had come from Dorset. He lived in the gamekeeper's cottage quite near Benedict's Pool with his wife, a tight-lipped, lean woman. They lived, it is true, at odds with one another and indeed had not spoken for years, ever since Jarvie made the fire up one dinner time.

"That's my job, leave the fire alone," Ada announced as she brought him a cup of tea at the fireside after dinner. Oh, she cooked and washed for Jarvie but they never spoke, living like a couple belonging to some silent order of monks.

Then one night, as Jarvie returned from the Cider Mill, a woman wished him "Good night". Jarvie said afterwards that the night was as black as the ace of spades. He didn't recognise the woman's voice at first. Well plied with Badger's cider, he instinctively replied, "Good night to you Ma'am." The spell had been broken. After that meeting Jarvie and Ada were friends once more, speaking across the kitchen table over their meals.

Jarvie and David Hicks, Tom Samson's gamekeeper, didn't hit it off. As Jarvie said, "We beunt exactly first cousins." Their feud started when David Hicks put strychnine down, mixed into corn on the headland of Tom Samson's bean field, to poison the rooks and pigeons. Why this affected Jarvie was because the crows, rooks and pigeons began flying over the next village of Alstone and falling dead in the road by the police station. The birds were trying to get to the wood by the monastery below Benedict's Pool. Jarvie was blamed for this by the village constable. He walked across the Hill warning David Hicks and there had been friction between the two keepers ever since.

Queenie White lived along with Jack Lampit in a little cottage in Lenchwick Lane a mile from Netherstone village. Queenie came there at the turn of the century and bought this pretty little cottage and took Jack in as a lodger. Queenie had a colourful past, but no one knew the real truth about her. It's sufficient here to say that she had been a lady, a Vicar's daughter from Norfolk, and that she had attended rather an exclusive girls' school — Queenie herself had it that she was educated at Girton. Her middle-class background did show. She spoke with a cultured accent, there was a certain character in her face and she undoubtedly had a presence of sorts. How she became associated with Jack Lampit was a mystery. Jack was a coarse farm labourer, of the worst order.

One thing they did have in common was their addiction to drink. Jack was a cider drinker, often walking home from the Mill in a drunken stupor, but Queenie liked her whiskey.

One particular Saturday night Queenie spent her evening at the Cider Mill while Jack was alone at the cottage. It was a bright moonlit night when Queenie took the footpath from there to Lenchwick Lane. There was a perfectly good road from the Cider Mill to her cottage, but the footpath was a full mile nearer.

As an old man, Jarvie Ricketts remembered that night on the Hill. Many years later we met and talked about those old times. Jarvie had been wakened by shouting and screaming as he lay sleeping in the gamekeeper's cottage. "Hark! There's someone in trouble," his wife Ada called and Jarvie arose from their bed, as he said, "All of a muck sweat." He called from the bedroom window. He heard the ancient call of "Man lost, man lost" but the voice was that of a woman in distress.

Jarvie put on his trousers and a coat and boots, lit a hurricane lamp and went out into the cold night air. "Where are you?" he called.

"I'm here," the voice cried from the centre of the field past Jarvie's garden.

Jarvie found Queenie but didn't recognise her even when he shone the lantern in her face. "There she was," he said, "a bald-headed lady in the moonlight. Have ever you seen a bald-headed lady in the moonlight?" I shook my head.

"What are you doing here?" Jarvie had asked her as he shook partly with fright and partly with cold.

"I've lost my wig down there in the water," she replied.

A little stream flowed on the Hill that fed a water tank where some of the cottagers obtained their drinking water.

"I want to get to Lenchwick Lane," she said when Jarvie had asked her in his quaint way, "Where are you steering for?"

As Jarvie followed the stream to the tank he found the wig floating on the water. Retrieving it, he shone his lantern towards Queenie as she replaced it on her bald head and then he noticed she had not got a dry thread on her. She had been in the water tank!

Jarvie walked with her along the footpath and pointed out to her that the tops of the trees on the sky line, if she walked that way, would lead her to the stone hill stile.

"Oh, I know where the stone hill stile is," she said and went on her crooked way, as Jarvie said "As drunk as a bob howlud."

Jarvie, in his time, had worked on a neighbouring estate where there was a deer path. Every Boxing Day the General, who owned the estate, gave the bell-ringers a supper and it was Jarvie who had to provide the venison. An Avion is a castrated stag, so when the fawns were born in the spring and were dropped in the bracken Jarvie would castrate several and mark them in some way. In the early winter Jarvie, with the aim of a true master at his craft, shot an Avion with a rifle on the Hill. He dressed it and when it had been hung it provided the venison for the supper.

Every winter Jarvie was in demand, killing and dressing the cottagers' pigs. One boar he killed was rather a challenge. It was a big Gloucester Old Spot. On his pig-killing rounds Jarvie often passed the farm where this old boar was kept in a sty and yard near the road.

Whether it was the smell of blood on Jarvie's clothes or not (and that's just one theory), the old boar roared at Jarvie like a lion. The animal had great long tusks and no one had dared to enter the pen for eighteen months to clean him out, his food being dropped over the fence. Mr Lister, who owned the pig, asked Jarvie if he would kill him. The pig killer agreed and enlisted one of Mr Lister's men to help.

"I went over to the General's estate where I used to be keeper and borrowed an army rifle and some ammunition. Now, as you know, pigs be partial to apples. So, I lent over the fence and gave him an apple. I rubbed another apple on my rope, the rope I lassoo the pigs with. As the old boar put his snout through the noose of the rope and was licking the apple juice, I pulled the rope and tied him to the railings and shot him. When I dressed him the bullet had gone half way down his back bone. He was maybe twenty score pounds in weight, no good for bacon. Bacon from boars of that age tastes like grit in your teeth. He could have gone for sausage meat."

Jarvie had some difficult ones to kill but none like Mr Lister's.

Another story Jarvie told me involved rabbits. "Have you ever been out with the long rabbit net?" he asked me. I admitted that I had but not with a lot of success.

One night, Jarvie explained, he had gone up on Fiddlers Knap. There was a big earth up there and he knew that the rabbits would be grazing down below. With his brother, he set the net, measuring about 100 yards long, some distance from a coppice. With four spaniel dogs Jarvie walked the Hill below the Knap while his brother was in charge of the net. When Jarvie arrived back at where the net had been set, it was gone! The weight of the rabbits that had come down the Hill had taken the net almost to the coppice, and Jarvie and his brother had taken fifty-two rabbits at the one draw.

"But that's nothing," Jarvie said with his wry smile.

"It's a lot of rabbits," I exclaimed.

"Well, on the thirtieth of August one year at the Park when I worked for the General we had a shoot. We cut the bracken in squares on the Hill. There were fourteen beaters and two guns to each square. As the rabbits bolted, 980 were shot that day and I hocked and paunched the lot!"

The fact that there was a ghost at Benedict's Pool was quite common knowledge. Joe the Hermit, from the barn near the Folly, would never go by the pool on moonlit nights. He and Jarvie had a common theory about the spookiness of this large pond by the Monastery.

Jarvie, who lived nearby, on his rounds as keeper passed the pond regularly on the footpath. He was coming home from work one dinner-time on a bright summer's day when towards him came a lady dressed in white. As they met Jarvie touched his hat and the lady said, "Good morning."

When Jarvie looked back along the path, the mysterious lady had disappeared. But the path was straight and there were no trees around. Jarvie looked left and right but saw no sign of the lady in white.

"When I got home I couldn't speak and had to take my hat off with both hands. Previously my hair was jet black but that day it turned white and I couldn't get that same hat on for a fortnight."

Jarvie lived to be over ninety years of age and when we last met, when I visited him in hospital, he said, "Some say that we come back to earth in a different form. It's called reincarnation. If I come back I'd like to return as a Cotswold ram and be turned up with forty ewes."

CHAPTER
FIVE

The Lady in Red

When Alfred, James or Jarvie were fearful of happenings on the Hill they usually went to see Joe the Hermit who lived near the Tower. Joe was a giant of a man, about six feet five inches tall with a build to match. No one or nothing upset the smooth-running day-to-day life of this remarkable man.

It was dinner-time when Alfred and James went to the barn by Parson's Folly where Joe the Hermit was frying liver over a wood fire, liver from a pig killed by Jarvie the previous day.

"You would like a bit of liver happen?" were Joe's first words as the brothers entered the barn. The pig hung from a beam to the earthen floor of the barn. Joe always called his pig Jesus; he didn't consider it that irreverent, it was simply the name he chose. The brothers sat together on a pig bench where yesterday's slaughter had taken place.

It seemed that the unexplained mysterious happenings on the Hill that so upset the brothers were soothed by Joe's unflappable life-style. What a contrast to Revd Cuthbert! But these two opposites were a tranquilliser to two simple men, the carter and the shepherd.

As the three men sat around the log fire in the barn Joe could see that the brothers had worries. He could sense it, in his peculiar way. "Now look yer," he began, "I been up on this hill alone for twenty years or more and never has anything happened to frighten me. You unt alone in being scared of some of the things unnatural. Jarvie the Gamekeeper who killed my pig yesterday, he's afraid to go too near to Benedict's Pool. Mind ya, the croaking of the frogs on a spring evening and the flops they make as they come from the water is eerie until you get used to it. I did see an otter there a while back. Jarvie often calls here. He's got his problems — that tight-lipped wife of his! That's something we three have never been troubled with. Mind you, Jarvie's one for the ladies. He seems to have a way with him, perhaps it's those bright blue eyes. The lady at Rings Castle depends on Jarvie on the night of the full moon. Her name is Frances and her husband left her and went to Birmingham."

The story that Jarvie had told Joe of the Lady in Red did nothing to settle the minds of the brothers. Joe continued with Jarvie's tale, a tale of forbidden love. "When the moon is at the full Frances goes up on the flat roof of the Castle, built by a smuggler who brought spices, tobacco, contraband up the Avon River and dealt in such things. Always a step ahead of the Excise Men."

The wailing and screaming of Frances from the roof of the Castle as the full moon rose over the Cotswold Edge had to be heard to be believed. Joe knew that Jarvie would soon be there to confirm the truth of the eerie tale — if he could get away from that wife of his.

Dressed in a bright red dressing-gown, standing on the battlements of the Castle, Frances was a picture in the moonlight. She would shout, "There it goes, there it goes, the stage-coach taking the contraband from the castle." Jarvie heard nothing but Frances said the sound of the horses' hooves and the rattle of the wheels of the coach driven by spring-healed Jack were real.

As Jarvie stood by her on the roof she would declare that she had heard the coachman's horn and, clinging to the gamekeeper, she would implore him not to leave her. But there was no fear of that for this Lady of the Moonlight had charm. Every time the moon rose full over the Cotswold Edge it was like Christmas Day for the sprightly little gamekeeper!

Frances was of an uncertain age, maybe fifty. Her red dressing-gown with a bright orange girdle was ankle length but was unable to contain her ample bust, which escaped from beneath the bodice of her orange silk night-gown.

The monthly pattern came as regular as the full moon. Frances would lead Jarvie down the spiral staircase, not to her bedroom on the first floor but to the snug sitting-room where the log fire burned brightly and the oil lamps flickered from the partly open window to the Hill.

"Madeira, my friend?" Jarvie would always nod as Frances poured generous measures of wine into crystal glasses.

In later years Jarvie said he could still smell the spices from the smuggler who lived in that place. The various happenings on the Hill and the local gossip during the month past were exchanged between the lovers on those evenings. Jarvie always exaggerated the news of the Hill, and Frances, living with her imaginings, told of her loneliness between his visits.

Ada, Jarvie's wife, was obviously suspicious of Jarvie's late homecomings on moonlit nights but, of course, he said there were traps to visit on the estate. One trap she never discovered was Frances, the Lady in Red. Oh, the gamekeeper called whenever he had the excuse inbetween the moonlit visits. On those nights, when the glasses of Madeira had been drunk and Jarvie had smelled the spices, the gamekeeper held Frances's ample breasts as the two lay on the gold-braided sofa in front of the log fire. Nature took its course, undeterred by the words of one of the Ten Commandments, and the two lovers slept until the early hours.

"The two most powerful things in the world are gunpowder, that will blow you up, and a woman, that will draw ya," was just one of Jarvie's theories, and he seemed to have proved it right.

CHAPTER
SIX

Changes on the Hill

It is surprising how things changed in the life of the village and the farm in just four years. Alfred Bullen had suffered from arthritis for ages but now things went from bad to worse. His brother James had always managed the ploughing on the Hill land but when Tom Samson bought some young horses from the horse fair the slow steady pace of Captain and Colonel was doubled by those younger beasts. In fact, Tom Samson had been left a small fortune by a maiden aunt. Obviously Ruth, his daughter, would benefit by this but agreed to the purchase of Park Farm, a hill property adjoining Sheldon. The house was empty and Tom had just the two Bullen brothers, now elderly, at Cobblers Quar. Tom therefore engaged a Welsh family, a couple with two sons, to work for him — Owen Pritchard and his wife Gwen and their two sons, Gilbert and Evan, who were twins and had just celebrated their eighteenth birthday.

The coming of the Pritchard family to Park Farm was not only a vast improvement to life on Tom Samson's farm at Sheldon but also a welcome addition to village life at Netherstone.

Gilbert Pritchard handled the young horses that Tom had bought with patience and skill. At eighteen he worked them like a man of experience. Four shire animals were a delight to see on Bredon Hill, two young mares, both in foal, and two jet black geldings.

At Park Farm the cow stalls and yards had been empty since the last owner left eighteen months ago. Owen Pritchard, an experienced stockman, went with his boss to the local markets where they chose dark red Shorthorn cows, some in calf, some in milk. Crossed with a young Hereford bull these animals would be the nucleus of Tom's beef herd. Young Evan Pritchard brought with him from Brecon his Border Collie sheepdog trained by himself. He took over the sheep on the Hill with Alfred as a part-time help; his experience would be invaluable at lambing time.

With a younger staff and younger horses Tom Samson was anxious to find work for James, his old carter who was now approaching sixty-five. Captain and Colonel, the two old horses, grazed the Leasowes, those two grassy fields above the Cuckoo Pen, but Tom Samson had ideas for their retirement. They were handy to catch in the morning and proved the ideal horses to pull the carts loaded with hay to fodder Owen Pritchard's Shorthorn herd. Old James used them in turn and he led the steady, trustworthy 25-year-olds as Owen loaded the hay and scattered it on the tops of the ridges of the field. It is true James had turned full circle, he was now the ploughboy, albeit an aged one, but he was more than happy to still be a part of Samson's team.

There is little doubt that the Pritchards from Brecon took the village by storm. Owen joined the bell-ringers at week-night practice and Sunday services. Gwen became assistant organist at the same church where the twins sang in the choir.

Ruth Samson had started music classes in what was known as the Ballroom, above Tom's nag stable. Gilbert and Evan were learning the violin, with Ruth on the piano, and dances became a monthly occurrence on those winter Saturday nights when the moon was full.

"Master Samson," young Gilbert said one morning as he led a couple of the geldings from the stable, "the two geldings, Boxer and Turpin, do plough an acre a day. They be good horses."

"So what?" their boss questioned. "I know you plough your acre, and don't tell James, but your plough turns over soil that has never seen the light of day before. You get deeper than the old team."

"When we were in Wales, Father used a double-furrow Cockshutt plough and he did do nigh on two acres in a day with a plough pulled by three horses. I fancy a plough like that, Sir, and I know from Father how to hitch on the team. The whipple-tree is offset and the furrow horse has the longer pull while the land horses the shorter pull."

Tom Samson pushed his peaked cap higher over his brow and thought, "We have got a young chap here with some knowledge." Turning to Gilbert, he said, "It's what is called fulcrum. I've seen it at work in Gloucestershire. I'm not promising a Cockshutt plough with two furrows but if you did fancy a three-horse team and the possibility of two acres a day, well, it is a thought."

It was Michaelmas when the Pritchards came to Park Farm so the mares bought in foal were still able to work until the New Year. They foaled in May.

Tom Samson had reviewed his lambing ewes all summer and decided that the Cotswold breed was not so popular in the market. Their lambs were heavy, producing big joints of meat. He decided that some Kerry Hill ewes crossed with a Downland tup, either a Hampshire or a Suffolk, would produce the lamb the housewife required.

The Cotswolds went to market as draft ewes that October. Tom Samson took the train to Knighton in Radnorshire, buying a flock of Kerry Hill ewes known in the trade as theaves, four-toothed animals. Evan Pritchard was delighted, Alfred was doubtful. The Kerrys were active but soon controlled by the young shepherd's dog, Skipper.

As the Suffolk tups were plastered with raddle every dewy morning that autumn, Alfred made the mixture and put the tell-tale paint on the rams' breasts as young Evan sat them up in front of him. Alfred, now sixty-eight, was supposed to be part-time but his life was with sheep and he followed the young man from Brecon, giving him tips that he had learnt as a boy. The old and the young made a good team.

David Hicks, the gamekeeper, who lived with his wife Patience at Camp Cottage, took over the shoot at Park Farm beside the woodland on the Hill above Netherstone. Old Jarvie Ricketts, now on the pension, lived with his memories and his garden. There had been friction between these two keepers because of David's dangerous practice of poisoning the pigeons and crows on Tom Samson's Netherstone farm. This had been resolved with a session, as it was called, at the Cider Mill Inn.

It was at meetings at the Inn that Jarvie and the other countrymen shared their secrets with one and all. David was as intrigued as the next man. Many years had passed since Jarvie raised the pheasant chicks and young partridges for the General at the Castle. Jarvie could be described as a man before his time. Like all the older countryfolk, he knew the secrets of the land. The puff balls that grew to a giant size on Bredon Hill were given the name of Puck Fice because they grew in fairy rings. These balls, when ripe in the autumn, when squeezed would make a cloud of brown dust like smoke. The dusty spores had been used by countryfolk to cure cuts and burns long before penicillin was thought of. The spores would also be used to calm a hive of bees, a type of early anaesthetic. Jarvie knew for a fact that a hot-cross bun kept in the chimney corner and mouldy after keeping for a year was good for a youngster with belly ache. These simple countryfolk may well have discovered the value of mould long before the advent of penicillin.

From Brecon, Owen brought with him much of the folklore of mid-Wales. When his Shorthorn cows calved in the field he was particular to throw the placenta, the afterbirth, what the Gloucestershire countryfolk called "the cleansings", onto a hawthorn bush. The hawthorn is commonly known as quick thorn, and it was believed that if the cow's afterbirth was allowed to decay on the quick thorn, it would leave the cow fertile for another calf.

James Bullen told of how one of his old horses, Colonel, came into the stable after a night in the fields, as he said, all of a muck sweat. His father had told him that the horse had been "hag ridden" by spirits and hobgoblins, and he had prevented this from happening again by hanging a hag stone, a flint with a hole in the middle, over the stable door to prevent the evil eye.

Old Alfred Bullen mopped his brow, called for a pint all round, and said, "There's things in this world we ain't intended to know about."

David Hicks, like all gamekeepers, was a solitary man who kept his own counsel. He and his wife Patience had a daughter of about eighteen, a slim, dark-haired, good-looking girl who worked as a nanny for a family in the Vale. She went to the music classes and the dances in the Ballroom, and there developed an attraction between Gilbert Pritchard, Samson's young carter, and this young lady from Camp Cottage.

"They be sweethearting," Alfred announced at the Cider Mill. Not that everyone didn't already know that the young couple were spending their leisure hours together — Alfred and James were often a little behind with the latest news on the Hill. Everyone was pleased by this new attachment, including the Parson.

Having extended his farm to Park Farm as the result of his Aunt's bequest in her will, Tom Samson had refurbished the nag stable at Sheldon and engaged a groom, who lodged at Sunshine Farm with Daisy Sands and her love child Sep, a ne'er-do-well who spent his time poaching and at the Cider Mill.

Ruth Samson was now nineteen and was living at home. She acted as her father's secretary, and dealt with all monetary affairs and the farm accounts.

Tom, his wife Sarah and Ruth were keen on hunting on the Hill and around the district. Tom had become Master of the local pack of hounds. A sight to behold, James Bullen declared as he admired the Gaffer on his weight-carrying hunter with Sarah and Ruth riding side-saddle on their hunters. Jack Ford, the new groom, was an ex-army chap who had served in the Royal Army Veterinary Corps. He looked after the small stable of hunters but worked on the farms at hay-making and harvest, in fact wherever and whenever he was needed.

As hunting took over more of the Samson family's time Owen Pritchard, apart from being stockman, became a kind of farm manager. What Owen said was what Alfred called "Gospel".

Nathan Brice lived near the Monastery below the Benedict's Pool. He had been saddler at Perry Cottage for years, he and his brother Jim following their father in that trade. Sarah and Ruth Samson both needed new side-saddles, bridles, and so on for their hunters. As Alfred Bullen said, "They be the family of the Master of the Hunt and can't be seen among the Gentry in any rag-tag tackle." Nathan Brice was delighted with the order for saddling from the Samson family. He was well into his seventies but Jim was ten years younger.

These bachelors, regular communicants at the Church, kept a maid and housekeeper, Bertha Brown, a spinster of nearly thirty-six, experienced in domestic matters and who had been employed by the Brices for many years. Like countrymen of that time their lives were steeped in folklore and superstition.

Just before Christmas, as usual, Jarvie Ricketts came to kill a bacon pig for the Brices. Nathan and Jim usually had a pig of sixteen score. After the butchering and the flitches being placed in the salting lead, Bertha apparently handled the bacon in the salt. Now call it either folklore, superstition or whatever, but that meat in salt should never have been handled by a woman, more so if that woman had what Jarvie called "the curse" or the monthly period. Brice's bacon went wrong, it never took the salt and was ruined. Poor Bertha, she got the blame.

"Have you handled the flitches?" Nathan Brice demanded of the housekeeper.

"Yes. I turned them in the salt lead," she confessed. Bertha was dismissed from her employment at a moment's notice and the Brices had to buy their bacon that winter.

Goodness knows why, but Jim Brice, the younger of the two saddlers, kept a white Shorthorn bull, which he grazed on the village green. It was a big lumbering animal, tethered on a chain on the green at the bottom of Rabbit Lane. Like the men who travelled the stallions to serve the shire mares, Jim took Satan, a devilish name for an animal, to the farms around when cows were what Alfred described as "In Use". Satan was a quiet Shorthorn and Jim could have lead him anywhere literally on a shoelace but, to be on the safe side, he had a leather strap and chain attached to Satan's ring.

When Tom Samson started his Shorthorn herd and crossed them with a Hereford bull he wasn't really interested in Jim Brices' Satan, but when replacements were needed at Park Farm Tom did call on Jim Brice for Satan's services with his best cows. Jim enjoyed walking that stately animal along the Netherstone road and up to Park Farm. He was glad to get away from the saddlers workshop for Nathan did the new work, making bridles and saddles, leaving Jim to mend cart harnesses and reline collars and mend the boots for the farm men.

Nathan referred to himself as what he called a Master Saddler and was proud to see the Samsons on their hunters dressed in his gear as they followed the pack.

What Nathan died of no one knew. He never had the Doctor, but one day Jim found him slumped across his bench, as Alfred said "as dyud as mutton". The funeral was arranged at Netherstone Church and Nathan lay in his wooden box in the sitting-room of Perry Cottage. Jim had left with Satan the bull, a call had come from Park Farm for his services. A spark from the log fire ignited a sofa near where Nathan lay in his coffin. Soon the whole of the black and white cottage was ablaze. Afterwards, a commendation appeared in the Parish Magazine explaining how the village fire brigade, with its antique equipment, had extinguished the fire. The magazine reads: "Had the fire been at the mercy of the brigade from a town seven miles away the whole cottage would have been destroyed." You see, the brigade in the town had to catch the horses to pull its fire engine. Those horses grazed the riverside meadows of the Avon and it took time for them to reach any of the villages. The village fire brigade, with its old-fashioned hand pump and a cider barrel on a pony cart, pumped water from the nearby brook onto Perry Cottage.

Meanwhile, it's worth a thought that had the cottage been completely burned down, poor old Nathan in his coffin may well have been unexpectedly cremated.

CHAPTER
SEVEN

Ruth's Visit to Cobblers Quar

It was during their mid-day meal at Sheldon on May Day that Ruth Samson told her parents that she was concerned about the two old bachelors at Cobblers Quar.

"They're quite happy there, Dear, with their garden and a pig in the sty and a few hens." Tom Samson smiled as he said that really there was not a lot of work for them, and it was true that Alfred did miss the Cotswold tegs that he used to hurdle on the turnip field. Now he helps Evan with the lambing, and James still dotes on the old horses Colonel and Captain.

"But Daddy," Ruth replied, "you know that Alfred and James have always worked for all the hours of daylight. They miss it badly. Can't you find them something more to do?"

Ruth's father thought deeply over his after dinner cup of tea, and finally replied, "Yes. There's that wall that has fallen down over by the long plantation where the mountain ash trees grow. I'll get them to rebuild it. There's a wire fence there at the moment, but the stone needs rebuilding. It was originally built, of course, at the time of the inclosures of 1783."

50

"Thank you, Dad. I'll ride over at tea-time and have a talk with them. They intrigue me, you know, with their Shakespearean dialect and their simple ways."

Geology and social history were still a passion for Ruth and she enjoyed talking and listening to the older folk of the area. Now an attractive girl of twenty, and with her father's book-keeping up-to-date, a ride across to Cobblers Quar was stimulating in the fresh air of that May Day.

She found Alfred in the garden moulding up his early potatoes, while James was planting a couple of rows of runner beans, making a little archway of nut sticks for them to climb in the summer

As Ruth slid off the saddle of her liver chestnut hunter, an example of Nathan Brice's artistry in leather and a saddle to be proud of, she called over the garden wall, "Hello there, you chaps are busy I see."

Alfred touched his billycock hat and replied, "Not too busy to make a cup of tea for you, Miss Samson."

"Can I tie Lively, my beautiful mare, to your apple tree?"

"Course you can," the men replied as one.

In the quite spacious kitchen a sway on pot hooks hung above a wood fire. James hung a big iron kettle over the glowing embers and gave the fire a good poke with his poker. "That ull soon boil, Miss. I could do with a drink, it's a warmish day. May Day, I gather."

"It seems to me that you and your brother miss the round of work on Dad's farm. I understand, but he has sent a message to say that the wall that has fallen down by the big plantation needs rebuilding."

"I be sure it does, Miss. The sight of a wire fence doesn't seem right on these hills of Cotswold stone."

"You are to rebuild it, Alfred and James."

This news brought a smile to the faces of the old bachelors. James, the younger of the brothers, said, "Alfred's a dabster at building dry stone walls and I be no novice."

Ruth looked at the two old farm men and saw the sadness in their faces. "It's a lovely spring day on the Hill, don't look so sad. It worries me."

"That's good on ya, Miss, but things be coming to pass on the Hill that seems like the vengeance of the Almighty."

"There's no such thing, Alfred, I'm sure, but as I've been studying the history of the Hill and the geology I have come across some mysteries. But that's life."

The kettle boiled and Alfred and James sat with their master's daughter round the scrubbed table drinking from half pint mugs, Jubilee mugs from the late Queen's Diamond Jubilee, a celebration of sixty years. The open fire was big enough to take two saucepans beside the iron kettle. One saucepan was for potatoes, the other one had turnip greens in it. James cut some bread and butter, and a pot of homemade jam given to them by the Pritchards completed their tea. The two men were generous. "You be welcome to stay to our cooked meal. We shall have some boiled bacon with the vegetables and some tea kettle broth."

"I must be home by eight o'clock, thanks all the same. That's when Mother cooks our meal, but this strawberry jam is very nice from Mrs Pritchard," Ruth replied.

When tea was finished Ruth began to tell the brothers a little about Bredon Hill. She began to explain that the rumbles they sometimes heard were part of an ongoing thing. The Hill is old, but not as old as the Malverns, and consists of lias and inferior oolite.

"That yunt very good news, Miss, anything inferior," James said taking in every word.

"That's just a term used in geology, James, but problems in subsidence do occur on the Hill at times and can cause cracks on the surface, but there's nothing to fear. I'm dead keen on geology, the study of the rock formations and landslips that have been going on for thousands of years."

"Thousands!" Alfred said, open-mouthed over his mug, "Parson Cuthbert reckons it's only six thousand years since Adam and Eve."

Ruth smiled. "Well, it's difficult to date things, but the Hill has a history of the Iron Age Camp, the Druids, the Romans, the Belgae tribes. You know, Alfred, many folks in the towns think that nothing happens in rural Gloucestershire, but you and I know that it does." Ruth was enjoying her time at Cobblers Quar, and still wanted to tell the brothers about the Hill's connection with the Gunpowder Plot.

"The taters be cooked and the greens. Fetch the bacon from the pantry, James. You don't mind us starting our fittle while we talk to you, Miss Samson?"

"I wonder what stories this old cottage could tell?" Ruth said quietly.

"Don't tell us nothing unkid or ghost-like, please Miss. We've already had one such experience at the Horse Camps."

"So I've heard. But really, you have nothing to fear."

Then Ruth told the Bullen brothers briefly why the Gunpowder Plot was celebrated by a bonfire every November.

"I know we do have a bonfire near to the Cuckoo Pen on 5 November, quite a party," James said with relish. "David Hicks and other men with muzzle-loader guns fire up into the air among those beech trees."

"What else happens?" Ruth was curious to know.

Alfred replied, "The Parson and his wife roast taters and apples in the embers of the fire along with sausages to be eaten with cottage loaves. All the folk from Netherstone and beyond go there."

"You know the history and why we celebrate? The plot to blow up Parliament was partly due to two men who had connections with Woolas Hall."

"Catholics I'll warrant," Alfred blurted out. "Our Parson don't hold with them and their ways, incense and the like."

James looked scared as he cleared the table. "Scared," he admitted, "to think we had such men only the other side of the Hill."

"It was the Winter family. Woolas Hall was a stronghold with a priest's hole to hide them from the Protestants."

"What happened to them, Miss Samson?"

"Well, they were hung, drawn and quartered."

"I'll go to Hanover! Hung, drawn, and quartered, butchered like cattle!"

"Not to worry. That was in 1606, and things have improved since then. Now there's more tolerance. But I

must be going, it's a quarter to eight. Come on Lively,"
she spoke to her mare, and the young lady cantered
across the Hill, behind the firs and the badger setts to
Sheldon.

The following week Alfred and James began rebuilding
the stone wall around the long plantation. A stretch had
fallen down, although in fact it had been happening for
years. The frost in winter, after heavy rain, played havoc
with the dry stone. Expansion and contraction followed
nature's rules — and the wall collapsed.

By June the sainfoin on the field by the Parish quarry
was in full bloom, a pink flower like a miniature
hyacinth. Sainfoin meant holy hay, and this hay was
favoured by the farmers for their sheep.

Tom Samson and his father before him had grown
about fifteen acres of sainfoin on the Hill for some years.
It was a persistent clover, which lasted about eight years.
In the rick by the barn when the haymaking was in
progress the scent of this holy hay was beautiful. It
needed harvesting carefully, without the aid of the
tedding machine which damaged the dried blossom.

A new two-horse mowing machine circled the field
that June day with the young geldings abreast on the
pole and Gilbert Pritchard on the iron seat. The work
started at first light and by mid-day Gilbert changed his
horses, putting the two young mares on the pole. James,
who still helped a little with the horses, took the two
geldings, lathery with sweat, to the shade of the stables.

There was very little left of the mowing by twilight as
Gilbert came to the stable yard at Sheldon with the two

mares. Both had foaled in May and the colt and the filly waited in the stable for their milk.

That evening being Saturday, Alfred and James took their weekly walk to the Cider Mill. There they met Jarvie Ricketts, Sep Sands and David Hicks.

"What do you think of your Gaffer's new mowing machine?" Joe Badger the landlord asked James, knowing full well that he wouldn't approve.

"'Tis like this, Joe. Master Samson's father and young Tom allus managed with the scythe. I know you younger chaps calls the scythe 'The Dismal', but when I was in the mowing team we mowed 100 acres one year."

"'Tis slow," Sep Sands said over his pint.

"Ay, and he's read the book alright," Alfred said with a gruff laugh.

"What book, Alf?"

"'Work and how to dodge it'. What do you fill your time with now the rabbits be out of season?"

"This and that," the young poacher replied. "I help Mother a bit on the farm."

"Bit's the name of it," Alf muttered.

"And there's a market for plovers' eggs in town. I get a couple of dozen most days."

"Well, to come back to mowing," James was anxious to make his point. "There's nothing under the sun so sweet as the sound of the swish of the scythe and the sight of the swath as it falls before the blade and turns colour in the sun. Now we allus was careful to protect the partridges' nest and we mowed around um, and the larks. Now that machine chatters its knife and fingers through the grass cutting everything. As the dew was on the grass those mornings with the scythe nothing broke the silence except the occasional sound of the whetstone on the blade. They got the binder to cut the corn these days. Days of Edward the Peacemaker. Well, the binder unt that peaceful like it was under the Old Queen when we cut by hook and by crook. It was hard work mind, with the bagging hook and pickthank to cut an acre a day."

Jarvie noted the conversation and, as an old gamekeeper, was very much against the horse-drawn mowing machine. Every partridge nest he could save was a bonus for him.

"When young Gilbert and Evan cuts the oats on the Hill who do you think cuts the road around the outside of the field?" Alfred queried, knowing that the young men could not cut with hook and crook and tie the sheaves. "I've had some harvesting mind," he added, "when the womenfolk tied the sheaves in straw bands with a Staffordshire knot. And I've had some wet shirts. I minds the time when I took my shirt off sopping wet and put it on the stooks to dry while I had me bait. Mind, the Gaffer was allus generous with some of his best cider, always a gallon a day."

Changing the subject, Jarvie said, "Have you heard of the ghost in Nettlestone. Some says that Nathan Price, as died a while back, has been seen round the Sally Coppice and that he's been leaving bundles of leather laces in a poplar tree. He's the only one who cut leather laces in Netherstone. His brother Jim has nothing to do with it."

"That's vengeance mind, since they sacked Bertha Brown over that bacon which went wrong. Vengeance is a powerful thing, especially when it comes from the One Above," Alfred said. "Parson said a Sunday 'Vengeance is Mine, I will repay saith the Lord'."

"I wouldn't take much notice of him, dressed like a woman and that collar on back to front."

"Mind what you say, Sep. He says he's God's messenger."

By Monday the sainfoin was half-made into hay and Tom Samson, with one of the young horses, turned the swathes then put the hay into walleye with a side delivery rake. As the sun shone, Gilbert arrived with horses and wagons and Owen Pritchard made a staddle with ash faggots to keep the hay off the ground. David Hicks and Jack Ford, the groom, helped to make up a team to gather the hay. David loaded the wagons with the hay pitched by Gilbert and Evan. Jack unloaded the hay to James Bullen on the rick, who forked it to Owen Pritchard, the rick builder. Alfred Bullen led the horses in the field, not forgetting to call "Hold tight" every time he went along between the walleys.

All seemed to go well that haymaking. Even Sep Sands reluctantly helped his mother and uncle to build a little rick at Sunshine Farm, helped by Jarvie Ricketts. Jarvie had a soft spot for Daisy Sands despite their age. Well, Jarvie fancied anything in a skirt!

In Daisy Sands' little meadow at Sunshine Farm half the hay had been carried and ricked. A hot sticky evening threatened thunder as the horse flies plagued man and beast and Daisy's few cows circled the paddock away from the bree fly, finishing up knee deep in her pool.

Queenie White had been having a session at the Apple Tree Inn, leaving at closing time quite drunk on Malvern Hill Perry. She stumbled part way home to Lenchwick Lane but rested a while in Daisy Sands' meadow, where some hay was still in the field. In the corner of the field Sep Sands had raked some of the fodder on the headland into a heap known as a cock. He had gone in to supper with his mother, uncle and Jarvie, but had left a jar of ale away from the sun in the haycock. As they sat down to eat Sep said, "I'll fetch that jar of cider, Mother, then Jarvie can have some before he goes home."

The sky had cleared after a few flashes of lightning over the Malverns, and half a moon rose over the Cotswolds. Sep walked leisurely towards the haycock. He wasn't used to a whole day's work and his uncle had set a fair pace in the hayfield. He fumbled for the jar of cider. "My God, it's moving! And I hear breathing." Sep was petrified. Queenie White's bald head popped up from under the hay. Her wig had either fallen off or she had taken it off to sleep. Sep screamed, and his mother rushed from the kitchen to see bald-headed Queenie emerge from the haycock.

"I don't know as I am frightened of ghosts," Sep told his mates at the Cider Mill later, "but that was real. I held her bald head in my hand thinking it to be my jar of cider. Then it moved and faced me."

Jarvie laughed loudly saying, "That proves what I saw near my cottage, not far from Benedict's Pool."

Despite his scare, Sep Sands told one and all that he didn't believe anyone had seen Nathan Brice since he died. Some said he was seen up Rabbit Lane where Jim used to parade the white bull.

"In Church on Sunday Parson Cuthbert said that there *are* spirits all around, good and evil and he's bin to Cambridge University." James's words reminded his brother of the time when Revd Cuthbert had arrived in the Parish from the University.

"Some of the lads, I won't say who, started calling after him saying he was a cissy to be riding that trike of his. Little did they know that Cuthbert got his Boxing Blue and he gave them a good hiding!"

CHAPTER
EIGHT

More Ghosts and Spirits at Netherstone

The news of Nathan Brice's ghost did make some folk afraid to walk the Rabbit Lane just west of Netherstone. More so because the lane was noted to be the haunt of spring-heeled Jack, an elf-like creature that had been seen by the sand pit.

As so often happens in life, stories get exaggerated and the dividing line between reality and the spirit world seems slender. It was a well-known fact in Netherstone that Groaten House was haunted. This Elizabethan farmhouse, half timbered with a cruck structure, had been unoccupied for many years. It was originally the Bailiff's house but the Squire could not find a tenant. The Prayer Room on the landing had often provided a refuge for Roman Catholics, Nonconformists and the like, depending on what sort of religion was the orthodox one of the day.

Eventually the Squire had found a bailiff from Somerset willing to live there, despite its history of ghosts and strange noises. He discovered that the hollow walls were like main roads between the timbers and the rats moved in, feeding on the corn ricks in the farmyard. So the story was one of rats rather than ghosts and spirits.

Alfred and Jim Bullen, however, were not convinced, believing that there was a ghost — that of Bill Aston, who had robbed the Sick and Dividend, or The Club, of over £100 and had fled to Canada where he died.

The story of the spirit world in Netherstone took a new turn when a young couple bought Higford House, a manor-type dwelling with massive stone balls either side of the gateway. Admiral Vernon once lived at Higford House. He was noted for his victory over the Spaniards at Porto Bello with only six ships. A medal struck in his honour in 1739 was found in the garden of Higford House in 1900. Admiral Vernon was known as Old Grog, as he dressed in a coat of grogram silk and mohair. He introduced rum rations for the Navy as a remedy for scurvy. His seaman's chest was kept in the Parish Church.

The young couple came to Higford House from Shropshire and were farming 200 acres of Vale land under Bredon Hill. They became very supportive of the Netherstone Church, and Revd Cuthbert, now an old man, was grateful for such folk.

The strange thing about the whole affair was that while Alice, the young farmer's wife, saw the ghost, her husband saw nothing at all. Alice first met the Naval Officer on the landing. He appeared whenever the full moon shone across the landing. He stood, in uniform, for a moment then went downstairs and disappeared. Neither Alice nor Frank had ever heard of Admiral

Vernon, but here they were confronted by, supposedly, the Admiral, who had lived there in the eighteenth century.

Revd Cuthbert was concerned that the young couple farming the 200 acres of land belonging to Higford House should be subjected to this thing he called a poltergeist. "There is one thing we can do," he told the young couple. "Get the house exorcised by the Bishop. I can arrange that, but first of all it may be wise to have a meeting, an open meeting, convened by the Parochial Church Council with the Churchwardens."

The vestry that winter's evening was packed with the parishioners of Netherstone. The two Churchwardens were Tom Samson and David Hicks. The meeting was chaired by Tom, who asked for everyone's opinion on the matter, calling first on Revd Cuthbert to explain what exorcism meant. Alfred and James Bullen, who had not yet got over their experience at the Horse Camps, trembled in their seats.

"Exorcism is one of the practices of the Church to expel Evil Spirits by invocation, or the use of a Holy name. Do you feel, friends, that we should help these young people, who are in a very frightening situation?"

Owen Pritchard said quite bluntly that he was not in favour of such a thing, coming as he did from a Nonconformist family from Wales. He believed that the Bishop, however Holy he might be, and he didn't doubt that, had no more power over evil spirits than the common man.

David Hicks said, "We are dealing with the unexplained and if the Bishop can get rid of the spirits, let him try."

"But if it is the spirit of the late Admiral Vernon, I fail to see that he is evil. He defeated the Spaniards at Porto Bello!" These words from Ruth Samson were confusing to folk like Jarvie Rickets and the Pritchards.

"There are spirits, evil spirits *and* good spirits, but they can all be frightening if not curbed," Joe Badger said, as he told of the faces of the Bullen brothers after their encounter with the spirits of Roman soldiers at the Horse Camps.

Alice Grove, the young farmer's wife of Higford House, then described what she had seen, always at full moon, on the landing. "This is not an evil spirit but nonetheless it haunts us. You see, often I have to go and settle my little girl. She's only four and sleeps in the little bedroom across the landing. But when the moon is full, this apparition stands before me. It is frightening, yet he seems friendly and goes away. His uniform is gorgeous but Frank, my husband, never sees him."

Tom Samson said he had an open mind on the matter. Then Revd Cuthbert asked for a vote. Apart from the Pritchard family, everyone was in favour of the Bishop coming to exorcize Higford House. Speaking for his family, Owen said, "We can pray for the young family and if we have faith the thing will go away without having the Bishop here."

As the majority were in favour the Vicar had permission to ask for the Bishop to visit. He came the following week and, accompanied by Revd Cuthbert and the Churchwardens, he invoked the spirit to depart.

But the feeling that night at Cobblers Quar was that it seemed that God was not pleased by the folk of the Hill.

Alfred and James went home with their candle lantern accompanied by Daisy and Sep Sands, who passed the Bullen's cottage on their way to Sunshine Farm.

Meanwhile — and no one knows why — Alice Grove never saw the Admiral again.

CHAPTER
NINE

Excursions

By 1907 excursion trains from Netherstone were commonplace on the old Midland branch line. Revd Cuthbert arranged parties from his church to explore previously unknown country. Only a few of his parishioners had seen the sea and the nearest coast town was Weston-super-Mare.

The first of these trips took place in September, after the Harvest Festival. The Pritchard family, David and Patience Hicks and their daughter, and the Bullens were among the party. It was a typical rural scene at Netherstone station when the train on the way from Birmingham to Weston stopped for its passengers. Alfred and James Bullen could be described as the star turn of the day. Dressed in their Sunday Best, each carried a frail basket with their mid-day meal and a bottle of cider. They were ushered into the carriages by the porter in his navy blue gear, all buttons and sleeve waist-coated. It was a corridor train, and Alfred was impressed when he saw the notice WC on one door. Exploring inside the little room Alfred, who couldn't read, shouted, "Here James, just thee read this yer."

James read carefully, "Not to be used when the train is standing in the station." It should be explained now that flush toilets were unknown in Netherstone. Alfred was very curious and as the train steamed from one station to the next, he pulled the chain.

"'Tis a good system," he declared, "but what about the men who work on the line? It seems to be a bit hard on them."

Back on the red plush seats in the carriage, the Bullens viewed the farming arena from their moving platform. Some land was flooded on the flat land of Somerset and blackened hay cocks still stood in the little fields. Small herds of milk cows were being milked in the fields, the farmer and his wife carrying their milking stools and buckets from cow to cow.

For Alfred and James, the first sight of the sea was like landing on another planet. The tide was in, what is called a "Spring Tide" the Parson said, but Alfred Bullen said that he must have got his calender wrong, 'twas September. The waves hitting the rocky shore sometimes came over the promenade.

The Pritchards, who had come from mid-Wales, had been on outings to Barry, taking the two boys there as toddlers, but as they told the Bullens, it's the same Bristol Channel there but on the other side.

"What do you think of it, Alfred and James?" David and Patience Hicks asked the brothers.

James took a couple of puffs at his pipe, pointed out to sea and announced for all to hear, "There's a lot of water out there, acres of it, enough for everyone. Parson says it ull be all gone back a mile in about six hours time." But the Bullens remained unconvinced until the tide actually receded.

In a shelter on the sea front Alfred and James opened their frail baskets, took out their cottage loaves and, with their bone-handled shut knives, made rough sandwiches of bread, cheese, boiled bacon and onions, swilling it down with cider.

"Any more for *The Skylark*?" a fat rounded chap in a fisherman's jersey said to the couple in the shelter.

"What sort of lark do you mean, Governor?" James replied. "I can't see any skylarks."

"Do you want a trip around the bay in my boat *The Skylark*? Half an hour for a shilling."

The two men of Bredon Hill shook their heads. "We be gwain to stop on dry land." But Evan and Gilbert Pritchard and David and Patience and their daughter took a trip. As they came back old Alfred said, "I be mortal glad to see them back on dry land, that boat reminds me of a rocking horse."

Revd Cuthbert had arranged for the party to have tea together at the end of the New Pier. Alfred Bullen looked longingly towards the land as the sea lapped below the floorboards of the pier. Owen Pritchard said he was surprised that the Bullens were putting their pennies in slot machines, especially the one that said "what the butler saw". Meanwhile, Revd Cuthbert said Grace before the tea, thanking God for a fine day and a safe trip on the train.

As the party boarded the homeward train and saw once more the Clifton Suspension Bridge, it seemed that the ones who had never had such a trip or seen the sea before had experienced as much as they could take for one day. Some slept on the comfortable sofa-like seats of the train, waking to see the gas-lit carriages and the street lights of Cheltenham.

"What do you think of the seaside?" Revd Cuthbert asked the passengers in his carriage. Together the Bullens announced that they would be happy to go on another excursion perhaps farther afield.

"It's all right for you," Evan Pritchard spoke with a hint of sarcasm. "You two old chaps are as good as retired."

"Don't forget," Alfred replied, "you will need me again when the ewes lamb in February."

"What trip have you in mind?" the Vicar asked James Bullen. "I see there's one to Scarborough in a fortnight's time. It's a lovely sea front I am told."

"How much, Vicar?"

"I believe it's six shillings, but it is quite a long way."

"We do like to see how the other farmers work their fields. We may go. What do you think, Alfred?"

"Oh, yes, we will go," Alfred declared, quite bitten with the new travelling bug.

It was early in the morning when the Bullens boarded the excursion to Scarborough. Like on their trip with the Vicar, they took their frail baskets full of provisions, but this journey was much longer and changing trains at York gave them an appetite. The bread, the cheese, the boiled bacon, were all eaten by the time the train eventually reached Scarborough station. When they changed trains at York and asked what platform the Scarborough train went from the porter had to repeat "Platform Four" — it sounded to these men of the West

Midlands as if he were saying "Platform Far". "You mean four!" James had got the idea.

Scarborough town was crowded with holiday-makers, the scenery was grand. "What about a bit of dinner now, 'tis one o'clock," suggested Alfred. "Just watch out, there's lots of eating houses along the sea front."

"Here's one." James noticed a chap with a rolled newspaper who was shepherding a flock of folk into a restaurant like sheep, and outside James read A GOOD DINNER FOR EIGHTPENCE. "Seems reasonable."

Alfred agreed and they sat together at a table with a kind of lino instead of a tablecloth. The food came along, roast beef, Yorkshire pudding and peas. The beef and Yorkshire pudding and the potatoes were quite good, but the peas, oh, the peas. The brothers grew peas in their garden, sweet and with a bit of mint fit for a king. These peas when prodded with a fork just popped off the plate. They were hard, yellow and old. As they came out of the restaurant James tapped the chap with the newspaper on the shoulder and said, "You tell all the folks you got peas in there as hard as bullits and you will soon fill the restaurant!"

The return trip from Scarborough left at six o'clock, and darkness crept like a thief over the Yorkshire countryside. "Don't forget we got to change trains at York," Alfred reminded his younger brother.

"Leave it to me. We shall come in on Platform Far." And they both laughed, but soon the diddley-do, diddley-do of the train as it sped along the rails lulled the Bullens to sleep.

They woke to a porter calling Liverpool — they had ended up in Lancashire! The chap who took their tickets told them that the next train south was early on Sunday morning but they could stay in the waiting-room. So Sunday morning came, and dinner time saw the two men finally arrive at their village under Bredon Hill, experienced excursionists but tired and with no wish ever to see the sea again.

Today we might hear the catchphrase "This is the Age of the Train", Oh, it has some credibility but surely the years before the 1914 war was the time when railway companies really served the travelling public. So many villages were served by branch lines that connected them with the main line stations. In fact, it was easy to travel to all the great cities of Britain by changing trains at the main line railway junctions.

It was a summer morning in 1987 when Gilbert and Evan Pritchard, accompanied by Jack Ford, took an excursion from Evesholme station to France. The early morning train, "The Milk Train", from Netherstone got the young men to Evesholme where they changed onto the main line for Southampton en route to Cherbourg. Not since Dick Miles rode his Penny Farthing bicycle 100 miles to London had there been such excitement in Netherstone.

The party boarded the cross-channel steamer at Southampton at mid-morning and rounded the Isle of Wight until out of sight of land. The time soon passed as the three young men, ignorant of travelling on the sea, marvelled at the great engine below and the foam of the

71

paddles that propelled the boat along. A few pints at the bar and sandwiches in the lounge and the travellers felt like real explorers.

Landing at Cherbourg at the edge of night they made their way to a boarding house all included in the fare. "A funny name for a place to stay for Bed and Breakfast," Evan said quietly among the chatter of French voices. "'Tis called a 'Pension'. Perhaps we be come to the wrong house."

His brother replied, "It may be for Old Age Pensioners!"

The next morning was taken up around the shops and the harbour of the town where a few bottles of wine and some cheap tobacco pleased all three. "We should be careful," they said to one another. "These yer French are said to live mostly on frogs." But the restaurant they chose to eat at before the ship sailed at twelve o'clock was to their liking and the veal was tasty.

"I shall have to water my pony before we get on board," Jack Ford told the brothers and sure enough in the middle of the promenade was a sign reading hommes. "That's French for Men's and there's the lavatory."

As they entered, they realised that three-quarters of their bodies would be left visible to passers-by. It seemed to the men that the builders had not finished their job. Gilbert, Evan and John stood in a line and laughed as men and women passed the privy quite unperturbed. "I can't go," one said after another. "We will have to wait until we get on the steamer and a bit of privacy." Which is just what they decided to do.

The journey across the channel was rough, some said it was choppy, and Jack Ford was very sick and said, between bouts when he wanted to die, "If this is choppy, God help us if it gets rough."

The Pritchards were just fascinated by the huge waves and the porpoises, which they thought were whales, following the hoary wake made by the paddles.

It was in the small hours of the morning that the excursion train arrived at Evesholme and the three men walked a long five miles to Netherstone in the half light of dawn. They were looked upon in the Cider Mill as adventurers going to France. Well, maybe they were.

CHAPTER
TEN

The Bundling Stocking

The courtship of Gilbert Pritchard and Jane Hicks of Camp Cottage became what is known as "serious". Keeping company had now become an engagement. David and Patience were pleased that Gilbert had promised to make their daughter his wife.

Gamekeeper David spent many hours in the woods in daylight and dark, and Patience made Camp Cottage what could be called a trysting place for the engaged couple. Jane was a nanny for Alice and Frank Groves' little girl at Higford House. She was a shy lass, very precise, well spoken and loved by all who knew her in Netherstone, and most important of all she loved Gilbert. She was proud of this young Welshman from the Brecon Beacons. She liked his dark smooth hair, his accent and his caring manner. He used to entertain both her and her mother during those Saturday and Sunday evenings at Camp Cottage. The monthly dances and social evenings in the Ballroom at Park Farm were memorable and Revd Cuthbert's Magic Lantern and his Phonograph, although they might be considered rather unsophisticated forms of entertainment today, were much appreciated by the folk of Netherstone.

Horses were Gilbert's pride and joy, and his turned-out team was a pattern for farmers and their men all around Bredon. Gilbert spent all his hours off work with his lovely Jane. Tom Samson, his generous employer, gave Jack Ford, the groom, instructions to let Gilbert ride one of the older hunters in the nag stable at Park Farm over to Camp Cottage after work on Saturdays. On Saturday evenings they often went boating on the river, Gilbert so masculine on the punt pole as it disappeared, sometimes seventeen feet, touching the Avon's unpredictable bed.

Time had passed and the Pritchard twins were now twenty years of age. Owen was proud of them both, but Gilbert, it is true to say, was the more adventurous. While he had marriage to his lovely Jane in mind, it could be said that Evan was married to his flock of Kerry Hill ewes, a stay-at-home after his work on the now larger estate.

I suppose it was a couple of miles over the Hill from Park Farm to David Hicks' cottage, a thatched dwelling in a little combe on the Hill overlooking Netherstone Church. Camp Cottage was well named, for here Cromwell had stayed on his way to the Battle of Worcester. Now it was a sweet little dwelling in an orchard of cider apple trees.

In the spring of the year David was busy with his rows and rows of pheasant chicks in coops with their broody hens. The chestnut tree in the middle of Straights Furlong was in bloom. The candle-shaped flowers, white with shades of pink, complemented the young pale green leaves of the tree. It was here that David would stand for hours with his gun on those spring days, sheltered from sight by a stack of wood faggots, waiting for the sparrow hawks that stole the pheasant poults. A board on a pole told the story of David's battle against predators. Here the carcasses of hawks, jays, magpies, stoats and weasels were exhibited to man and beast, a talisman that said, without a word, "Here are the enemies of my chicks". Of course, when the coops were closed at night-time the broody hens foster-mothered their little family in relative safety. David had bought these broodies from farms and cottages in the Vale, four shillings being the going price for birds that would hatch out a dozen chicks in three weeks.

At night-time in the woods, and Straights Furlong adjoining, David watched and listened as nature unfolded — the cry of vixen with cubs to feed in the earths on the Hill, vixen willing to take a chance with a broody hen for the cubs supper if only she could tip over a coop and steal the broody.

David took no chances. He patrolled his territory on those vital spring nights. Sometimes he lay on an old sofa in a hut under the chestnut tree. So, Patience Hicks was lonely on Bredon in the spring. Gilbert would bring Jane home from the Saturday night dances at around eleven o'clock then ride back over to Park Farm. Patience felt so secure with Gilbert around, if only he could stay overnight. "We have only two bedrooms, both with double beds. If we had another, Gilbert could stop over until Sunday morning," she thought.

On a Saturday night in May Gilbert and Jane had arranged to attend a dance in the Ballroom over Tom

Samson's hunting stables. A lot of the young folk on and around the Hill were going to be there. Patience Hicks invited Gwen Pritchard over from Park Farm for tea and supper. Owen was busy with the spring calves at the farm but would fetch Gwen back home in a pony and Governess car at eleven o'clock with young Gilbert.

Patience and Gwen had had an evening of women's talk, both happy that the two families would be united one day. Patience was eager to know of Gwen's life on the Brecon Beacons, as a child and then as a young girl in service, and her Chapel upbringing. "Did you know Owen for long before you married?" Patience asked.

Gwen replied, "It depends on what you mean by 'know', Patience. We were engaged for two years, that's normal I suppose, but we had known each other since school-days. Courtship in Wales, Patience, is different in a way from England. It was very strict and if a young man and woman were even seen together the girl was considered a brazen hussy. When I was courting with Owen and was in domestic service he was only allowed to go as far as the Churchyard stile and watch me go to the farm where I was employed and hear the farm gate close."

It seems that this restriction was a lasting reminder of the rights of parents to choose partners for their children. Patience was intrigued by the old customs, but when Gwen told her of another custom that seemed quite contrary to this clandestine manner she was taken by surprise.

"Have you heard of bundling and bundling stockings, Patience?"

"No, Gwen, that's something I know nothing about."

Gwen hardly knew how to start, and became quite flushed in the face. Finally she said quite firmly, "I have done bundling and I have a bundling stocking. The custom is that when a couple are engaged to be married they go to bed together in their clothes and the girl wears a bundling stocking. The idea, and I believe it to be a good idea, is that the couple might get some idea of each other without taking any liberties. Touch played the part of sight in the unclothed."

Patience didn't know whether to laugh or cry. She was so emotional; a vivid imagination had always been one of her traits. "What's the stocking made of, Gwen?" she said at last and Gwen told her how she had knitted this protective garment herself from pure Welsh wool.

"I've still got it in the back bedroom in the bottom drawer of a chest. Jane can have it willingly if she wishes."

"Oh Gwen, you may have solved a problem when David is working these nights and I long for Gilbert to stay overnight." Patience put her arms around the Welsh woman and kissed her. "Never have I had such an interesting evening. It's eleven o'clock and here comes your husband with the horse and Governess car."

There was just time for Owen to have a drink after he'd tied his pony up on the iron ring at the end of the cottage, where Oliver Cromwell is said to have done just the same thing over two hundred years ago. It was eleven thirty when Gilbert and Jane arrived at Camp Cottage having come home in a brake with two young couples from the next village.

Owen Pritchard with Gilbert and Gwen in the Governess car were late travellers to Park Farm that Saturday night. What Owen's thoughts were, or those of his son, was anyone's guess, but Gwen had memories of bundling in bed and her bundling stocking. The night was silent with a silence that could be felt — a lovely spring night with the nightingale singing his heart out down by the osier beds near Benedict's Pool.

CHAPTER
ELEVEN

The Meet and After

As Master of the Bredon Fox Hounds Tom Samson had a Boxing Day Meet at his farm at Sheldon. Of course, since the bequest of his maiden aunt, Tom was now farming much of the land where the two counties, Gloucestershire and Worcestershire, meet. Sheldon was known as the home farm, and it was here that Jack Ford was in charge of the hunting stables.

The Meet was at ten thirty and although the days were short those winter meets were often memorable for the Samson family. The Bredon Hounds were a modest pack and the followers mostly small farmers from the Hill country, although some came from the other side of Parson's Folly.

Ruth Samson accompanied her mother as the hounds made for their first draw at Fiddler's Nap, a clump of beech trees below Parson's Folly tower. The two ladies riding carefully, their hunters beautifully groomed by young Jack Ford, were a picture as the golden sun peeped over the Cotswold Edge. Ruth Samson had grown into a very desirable lady with a lot of charm. Old Alf Bullen, now in his seventies, said, "Her's like one of us."

As Tom Samson was now farming more land he increased his staff and Ruth spent more time in the farm office dealing with accounts and wages. Alfred and James, who still worked part-time on the farm, talked of when the wage was ten shillings a week but now it was sixteen shillings, but when Alfred did overtime, as he reminded his brother, he often had a golden sovereign. Now the two old retainers from Cobblers Quar walked up to the Meet at Sheldon admiring the hunters and the Pink of the Huntsmen and Jack Ford, who was whipper-in.

As the field approached Fiddler's Nap a young man on a silver grey mare came from the direction of the Banbury Stone. "Sorry not to make it to the Meet, Mr Samson, but we have had problems with a calving cow, a heifer in fact."

"That's all right, Henry," the Master said to Henry Fairfax, the youngest son of old George Fairfax over in the Avon Marshes, good grassland where the cows would be grazing a month before the neighbours in the spring.

Tom introduced Henry to his wife and daughter and from that moment Henry took more than one glance at Ruth Samson. Henry had recently left agricultural college. The older members of his family were all married already, the brothers having farms of their own. This left Henry with Old George, now a widower, to work the farm.

A strange thing about hunting on Bredon was how it taxed the hunters, some carrying fat, overfed men of seventeen stone. The cantering across the flat of the Hill was fine, but if the fox made for the river valley and then decided to head for the summit of the Hill once again, the horses became tired. Alongside the river lay the osier beds, which provided the raw materials for hurdle making, and the sedges, used since the fourteenth century for making the frail baskets that every farmworker used for taking his morning bait and in which the carter would carry his plough spanners, shut links and so on for plough repairs.

This Boxing Day was no exception. Renard took a line from Fiddler's Nap down the Hill to the river valley. The followers on horseback went steadily down the steep escarpment of Bredon towards the river. Tom Samson's hounds were chivvying the fox in Henry Fairfax's osier beds, where the water from the Avon was knee deep. The hounds went on a View Halloo from a cottager on the hillside, and this was a signal for Tom's pack to follow the steep slope of the Hill.

"You're on your home ground, Henry," said Tom. "Are you following up the Hill again?"

Henry looked at Ruth on her light-weight hunter and pretty as a picture and nodded. It was three o'clock and soon the sun would set behind the Malverns, but what's an hour when you fancy you are in love.

By four o'clock, after many hold-ups, the hounds followed the fox through the wooded hillside and Ruth Samson and Henry Fairfax made a diversion in the rides of the woods. Sarah, with neighbouring farmers' wives, was at the Tower before the young couple. Renard had gone down an earth where the earth stopper had failed in his duty and the hunting horn gave the familiar music of "Gone to ground".

It was too late and darkness was now creeping on like a thief. Renard would live to run another day. The earth stopper who failed to close the fox's hole was Jarvie Ricketts who, like the Bullens, had seen too many Boxing Days, but hc had promised David Hicks to close the earth on his side of the Hill. As the huntsmen took the pack to the kennels of Furze Woodland, west of Bredon, Tom Samson jogged across to Sheldon with Sarah at his side. "I suppose she will be all right, although it is getting dark," he said to his wife.

"Ruth knows her way home, don't worry Tom," she replied.

Ruth and Henry were back near Fiddler's Nap and the hermit from Parson's Folly said that he saw them saying "goodbye" and looking very friendly. In fact, the two young folk were making plans to go to a dance the following Saturday at Cheltenham Town Hall. The main line railway station at Bredon provided an ideal service, a late train could take the countryfolk home, and Ruth arranged for Jack Ford to meet her in a trap.

On the Saturday morning in January when Henry Fairfax had arranged to meet Ruth Samson at Bredon station, the sun shone all the morning. "How lovely," Ruth remarked to old Alf Bullen, who touched his cap respectfully.

"'Tis a weather breeder, Miss," he replied looking up at the blue, cloudless sky.

"What do you mean, Alfred?"

"It's unseasonable for the time of year and we shall have snow in May happen."

After lunch at Sheldon Jack Ford took his master's daughter in the horse and trap to the railway station for the two o'clock train. Henry Fairfax was standing on the platform and greeted Ruth with a gentlemanly handshake. "I've got the return tickets," he announced, which brought a smile to the face of this attractive young lady. When the train arrived the porter opened the door of a first-class carriage for the couple.

"Henry, you shouldn't have paid first class. I've never travelled first before."

"It's a special occasion, Ruth, so why not celebrate."

The red plush seats of the carriage were warm from the heating system of the Midland Railway and soon the train arrived at Lansdown station, where Henry hailed a cab to take them to The Promenade.

"It's a shame the shops in The Promenade are closed on Saturday afternoon, but we can do a little window shopping," suggested Ruth.

"Never mind, Ruth. We will come, if you would like to, one day in the week when the rather up-market store is open."

Round the corner in High Street, at George's Restaurant, afternoon tea was being served. A quartet played waltzes and overtures, which set Ruth's feet tapping. She loved to dance and Henry was not to think that he was the first fellow to take Ruth out to tea. The couple lingered and chatted, telling one another about their experiences and interests. He told her about his time at the agricultural college and Ruth about her interests in geology and history.

Up the High Street, the Plough Hotel was open at six o'clock. "We have just time for a drink before the dance at the Town Hall," Ruth's escort said with some caution.

"There is a lounge there, apart from the public bar, if you don't mind meeting a few of my friends."

Sizing up this farmer and feeling her way without being too eager or too cool, Ruth simply said, "That's all right. You have time for a beer and a sherry will suit me."

At the Town Hall the orchestra had come from Bristol for a special New Year Ball. It was soon evident to Henry that Ruth Samson was a pretty proficient dancer and the couple took the floor almost every time the orchestra struck up the time-honoured tunes. Towards the end of the evening Henry introduced Ruth to a couple of his college friends and each took their turn, dancing the evening away. Finally it was time to leave. "It's quite a step to the station and the ten thirty train," Henry said. "Shall I get a cab?"

"No," Ruth smiled. "Let's walk up The Prom under the gas lights. It will be so romantic."

Henry squeezed her hand and said softly, "Can I call you Darling, for tonight has been heaven to me."

Ruth replied, "Yes, Dear. We hardly know each other yet, but life can be so special with a friend."

Jack Ford and his horse and trap were waiting at the station to take Ruth to Sheldon. Henry's farm was walking distance away but he was loath to say his goodbyes on Bredon platform. As they kissed under the oil lamp of the station the train continued its journey north to Birmingham. Henry and Ruth had begun their romance.

* * *

After Church and Sunday lunch Ruth walked from Sheldon to Cobblers Quar where the Bullen brothers were sitting by their wood fire. "I love the smell of wood smoke," Ruth said as she was invited into the cottage.

"Yes, Miss," James replied, "but never put elder wood on the fire, or the Devil will come down the chimney."

Ruth thought a while that here on the Hill early in the twentieth century folklore was nearer than was sometimes realised. James spoke of imps and spells, and how they were hidden away in cottages. Folk medicine was interwoven with religion, and Satan was someone to fear. As Alfred said as he lolled in his fireside chair, "Satan was seen only last week, came through the bedroom window at Groaten House and left a smell of brimstone when he went. The place lit up and there was no candle."

Ruth tried to console the two old men, yet she thought "Perhaps these beliefs are a part of their thinking, handed down from generations — the old beliefs that Satan, who Alfred calls Pecked Ears, is responsible for bad feelings and that witches have power in their spells."

James said, "You have heard of Daisy Sands and young Sep when they were at dinner one day last week?"

"No," Ruth replied, all ears as they say.

"Well, you know that there are travelling women who are witches?" Ruth nodded. "One went to Sunshine Farm as Daisy and Sep were having a meal and asked Daisy for some taters. Daisy said she was sorry but there was only enough for herself and her son. That was last Monday and the witch said she was casting a spell and they would never eat taters again. Now all last week Daisy couldn't eat her taters."

Ruth gave each of the brothers a tin of tobacco and left them with their thoughts. Her thoughts, meanwhile, were of a farmer from Bredon, of whom she was already rather fond.

CHAPTER
TWELVE

Back at the Cider Mill

Alfred and James Bullen usually managed to get to the Cider Mill on Saturday nights. It was here in Joe Badger's bar, and at Church on Sundays, that the brothers met the Netherstone folk. Cobblers Quar cottage was isolated on Bredon Hill. An oasis of solitude, the cottage stood in a walled-in garden with a deep well of spring water at the back of the wash-house. At closing time at the Cider Mill, Joe Badger put his pony in the spring cart and took the old men back to their cottage. Joe drove around the Hill, then up Pigeon Lane near Benedict's Pool to Cobblers Quar. The Bullens had arrived at the inn by a footpath through the woods.

With their tongues loosened by cider, Alfred and James told of their visit from Ruth Samson and how she had met Henry Fairfax at the Hunt on Boxing Day. "Call it gossip if you like, but the hermit at the Tower saw them saying their goodnights at Fiddler's Nap as the sun slipped over the Malverns. And they have been to a ball at Cheltenham. Jack Ford took Ruth to catch the train and to meet Henry at Bredon station."

"What's wrong with that? They be both unmarried young folk," Sep Sands said. Sep wasn't interested in the conversation. He had never wanted a girlfriend. His life consisted of poaching on Tom Samson's estate, and selling rabbits and a few pheasants from the woods where David Hicks was gamekeeper.

Tom Samson turned a blind eye to Sep's petty crimes; he knew that as this was his illegitimate son, it was a wise move. Daisy Sands, Sep's mother, on her little holding known as Sunshine Farm, was supported in a way by her former lover. Sep knew just how far he could go, and walked the bridle paths to town with his illegal bag selling the game in one of the pubs then returning by train to the Cider Mill. It could be said that Sep led a wasted life but he knew of his origins in the hayfield at Sunshine Farm when Tom Samson's heifers had got into Daisy Sands' meadow. "He's me father," he often said when the subject came up at the pub. Sep felt an outcast and drank heavily of Joe Badger's cider.

David Hicks came into the pub that Saturday night. He rarely drank in the village and left after a couple of pints around the log fire with the Bullen brothers. After he had gone, Jarvie Ricketts arrived. His cottage was only one field away.

"What bist drinking, Jarvie?" James questioned. "The cider's good but perhaps you prefer a beer."

"A cider for me. Cheers, James," and another of Tom Samson's old hands joined the Bullens and Sep Sands.

Alfred, now talkative, and Joe Badger and his wife, eager to hear news, good or bad, from the brothers, said in no more than a whisper, "Hast y'eard about Gilbert Pritchard and young Jane Hicks?"

"Course everyone knows they be courting," Jarvie said. "And why not?" he added.

Alfred sipped at the cider in his mug saying, "Courting you says, they be as good as married."

Sep, now rather amused by Alfred's insinuation and thinking to himself "I suppose we have got to put up with these old cronies on Saturday nights", blurted out, "They are engaged, so what?"

"That's not all," James spoke firmly. "They sleeps together on Saturday nights at the Camp Cottage. There's only two bedrooms in that cot and two double beds. Queenie White who does Patricia Hicks' washing says there's only two double sheets on a Monday."

Jarvie Ricketts, a man who knew more about the ways of women than most men, said, "Joe, I'll have another pint before I walk back home, and I'll tell you all about Gilbert and young Jane. 'Tis all above board, Gwen Pritchard told me and the missus about it last week. Gwen comes from the Brecon Beacons in mid-Wales and has brought some of the old customs with her. One old one is bundling."

"What's that got to do with single folk sleeping together?" Alfred replied.

"Well, of course you two old bachelors will never understand, but I'll tell you what Owen said. Gilbert and Jane sleep together in their clothes. It's a custom where engaged couples can get to know each other. Gwen said touch plays the part of sight and the girl wears a bundling stocking to cover her lower parts. The Welsh women knits these stockings and Gwen has given hers to young Jane. Ain't that better for him to stay the night at Camp Cottage with Jane while David's out in the woods as gamekeeper? And yunt that better than having bastard kids?" At this, Sep Sands looked purposefully at the older man, realising that if Queenie, his mother, had had a bundling stocking he would not have been around.

"Come on chaps," interrupted Joe, "I got the horse and cart ready to take you home." And the Bullens took their places beside the landlord of the Cider Mill and they headed for Cobblers Quar, their education duly extended even past their seventieth birthdays.

CHAPTER
THIRTEEN

Threshing Daisy's Barley Rick

Daisy Sands of Sunshine Farm grew one field of barley on her land, enough for one day's threshing. Her brother-in-law planted Spratt Archer, a good milling barley, and when the corn was ready for harvest Tom Samson sent Gilbert Pritchard with his binder to reap the field.

With much persuasion Sep helped his uncle to carry the sheaves on a wagon borrowed from Tom Samson to the rick yard. It took the two men a few days to build a reasonable rick standing on staddles in the yard. Daisy's brother-in-law and Tom Samson helped this widow for harvesting, and she kept some of the threshed barley to feed her hens, cockerels and geese. "They keeps her afloat," Alfred Bullen said, but in fact, Daisy was an able business woman and no mean farmer.

After harvest, when Tom Samson's corn was ricked and thatched in the rick yards of Park Farm and Sheldon, Daisy's rick stood under a tarpaulin sheet ready for the thresher. A steam engine from nearby Alstone and one threshing machine served the community, half a dozen small farmers around the Hill and, of course, Tom Samson's wheat, oats and barley. The problem with Daisy's farm was that it was approached by a steep track up Pigeon Lane. It took three of Tom Samson's horses, with Owen Pritchard, to pull the steam engine up the hill and two more with Gilbert to take the machine known as the threshing box to Sunshine Farm. However, all was ready the evening before the big day when the engine driver had steam up by seven o'clock.

Every year the same, a scratch team threshed Daisy's rick. The Pritchards did the heavy work, Gilbert wheeling the heavy sacks from the machine to Daisy's granary. Evan and Sep tossed the sheaves to the machine where James Bullen cut the strings off the sheaves and dropped them in front of the engine driver. Jack Ford helped Owen to build the straw rick with boltins tied neatly by two bands from the machine. David Hicks pitched the boltins of straw to the rick builders.

Daisy had asked Jack Lampit to help that day and he arrived late to carry the chaff from the machine into the barn. Jack wasn't happy. "Why should I have the dusty job with the thistles sticking in me collar, carrying sheets of chaff?"

Old Alfred Bullen smiled as he carried buckets of water with a yoke across his shoulders to quench the thirst of the steam engine. It was a little way from Daisy's well to the rick yard but Alfred managed to fill the half hogshead barrel that stood beside the engine, which sucked like plough horses at the trough, and the hose-pipe always found plenty more as Alfred kept up a continual trek back and forth to the well.

As dinner-time came, the great leather belt from the engine to the machine slowed down and flapped where the leather thongs joined it together and the engine puffed its last clouds of smoke and steam from the tall chimney. The engine driver had pushed the lever control to off and, after one last cough from the engine, the rick yard was silent. The little rick of Daisy's was half finished and the straw rick grew as the threshed straw made a sizable stack.

There was dust everywhere that Michaelmas Day. The men coughed and grumbled as they finished their bottles of cider. Jack Lampit, who wore a navy blue gansey over his Oxford shirt, had collected so many barley awns or ails, which stuck to the woollen garment, that he looked like a golden porcupine. "You can laugh, you ignorant oafs," he yelled at the Pritchard boys as he passed them going into the barn where Daisy had provided bread, boiled bacon and tea.

"No cider, Mrs?" Jack said, trying to pick the ails from his gansey.

"No, Jack," she replied. "We don't want any accidents with machinery around."

By six o'clock the rick was threshed, the straw built into a tidy stack, and the sacks of barley stored in the granary. Meanwhile, another chap had been working all day mending the gate to Daisy's garden, Jack be Nimble they called him. He used to recite that nursery rhyme about himself: "Jack be Nimble, Jack be Quick, Jack jump over the candle stick."

Jack was what was known as a rough carpenter. He could make and mend ladders and hurdles, put a shaft on a wagon, a general handy man. Tom Samson often employed him, but Jack was too fond of the drink to hold down a regular job. At the Cider Mill a quart pot was kept especially for him. He said he could not waste time on a pint. Jack came into Daisy's barn carrying his workman's tools in a carpenter's bag, his chisels, hammers, and his very sharp axe, which he had threaded through the two handles on his work bag that hung suspended behind his back.

By now, the Pritchards and David Hicks had gone home. Jack Ford, Sep Sands, Jack Lampit and Jack be Nimble sat on the sacks of barley in the granary. "What's in those two barrels?" Jack Lampit asked of his friends. Jack was thirsty, covered in barley ails and miserable.

"'Tis cider, belongs to Joe Badger. He's got it here in the cool now his cellar is full."

"I could down a few pints of cider and there we be, two barrels in granary and both untapped!" Jack Lampit had not had a good day, tired after carrying sheets of barley chaff to the cattle yard, his throat parched with dust, not to mention those pesky ails.

But Jack be Nimble smiled. He carefully placed his carpenter's bag on the floor of the granary, and groped inside for a small tool. "Here it is!" he said with a grin, and held up a bradawl, or what he called a nail paster. "I can drill a small hole in the cider barrel and we can sample Joe's agricultural brandy!"

Joe carefully bored a hole until a few drops of cider weeped out. He then got a clean straight straw from the threshing and put it into the hole and started sucking the strong liquid. "'Tis a drop of good drink," Jack be Nimble said, and he should know having drunk enough in his time to float a ship.

Sep and Jack Ford put straws through the hole and sucked the cool cider. Then Jack Lampit, who was probably thirstier than the rest, sucked away at the barrel until his face turned red.

"Half a minute," Sep whispered, the granary being close to the farmhouse where his mother was preparing tea. "Don't make a pig of yourself, Lampit." But Jack Lampit made sure of his ration.

In turn, Jack be Nimble, Sep and Jack Ford sucked who knows how many pints from the barrel. It seemed that Lampit had sucked cider through a straw before, but still it began to tell on him. He became quite talkative between his turns at the barrel.

It was seven o'clock when Sep and Jack Ford went into the farmhouse for tea with Daisy. "You been drinking?" she questioned.

"The engine driver gave us some cider from his costrel barrel before he went home," Sep, always ready with a lie, replied.

"Your tea's ready," was Daisy's sharp answer. She was for ever trying to reform her son from his heavy drinking.

Jack be Nimble left the granary with his bag of tools and walked unsteadily down the hill to his lodgings, leaving Lampit still sucking cider with a straw from the barrel. At last the drink got the better of him and he slumped onto a bed of straw by the barrels and was soon asleep.

Queenie White, known as his lieby, was worried when her man had not returned by eight o'clock. She walked up the hill to Sunshine Farm, quickening her steps past Benedict's Pool where the thought of ghosts played on her mind. When she arrived, Daisy, Sep and Jack Ford had finished their meal in the kitchen. A heavy knocking at the back door brought Daisy from her chair. "Who canst that be, Sep? 'Tis late."

"Oh, Daisy," Queenie blurted out. "Where's my man, Jack?"

"I'nt he gone home? Where is he, Sep?" Daisy was anxious and Queenie was dreading what could have happened to him.

Sep replied in his don't care way, "He was in the granary when we left."

The two women, followed by Sep and Jack Ford, rushed to the granary. As they opened the door in the twilight of Michaelmas evening guttural sounds came from a heap of straw. Jack Lampit was, what Daisy called, driving them home. His snores were sounds the four folk at Sunshine Farm will never forget.

"My poor dear," were the cries of Queenie White as she put her arms around her man and kissed his bristly face. "Are you very ill, Jack?"

Jack Lampit came too and exclaimed, "Where be I, is it a dream?"

"No, Dear," Queenie said. "I think he's had a seizure." Sep winked at Jack Ford, knowing full well what had overcome Lampit. "Can you stand?" Queenie asked holding his arm, and Jack Lampit stood shakily in the gloom of the granary.

"Where be I? You will have to take me home."

At length the truth came out that the men had been sucking cider through a straw. No one knew how much they had drunk, nor why sucking cider through a straw makes a man drunk sooner than drinking from a mug. Daisy, a good-hearted woman with a sense of humour, took Queenie and Jack Lampit into her kitchen and made a pot of tea. Jack sobered up slowly after a couple of rounds of Daisy's home-made bread and a hunk of cheese.

The harvest moon peeped over the Cotswold Edge like a ball of fire, lighting the Hill and casting shadows from the beech trees. Late in the evening Queenie White piloted Jack Lampit back to Lenchwick Lane. "Oh, Jack," she said, "we have to pass Benedict's Pool and things happen, you know, when the moon is full."

"Don't fret, Queenie, I be alongside you, nothing to be afraid of. You frightened Jarvie Ricketts you know, when you lost your wig."

Queenie gripped Jack's hand through the woods above the pool. The owl hooted, the rabbits scuttered to their burrows, and a badger crossed the ride. These were natural things that had happened since time began, but what of Benedict's Pool?

As the couple took the footpath past the water the mallard quacked, being disturbed on the pond. Fishes, great carp, rose and plopped on the water, and the moon reflecting in the water made everything look double, but the couple were soon home.

Queenie hugged her man on the leather sofa and took him upstairs to bed early. What happened as they settled together over the feathers we can just leave to the imagination. They were lovers in a very simple and rural way.

CHAPTER
FOURTEEN

The Earth Moves

On the boundary of Tom Samson's estate, the adjoining field, known as the Blackberry Hill, belonged to the General. The hill covered with blackberries was a mecca for the women of Netherstone when the berries were ripe in August. None knew why, but these flat bushes grew fruit very similar to the cultivated variety.

Apart from these blackberry bushes, gorse grew in abundance and the rabbits were permanent tenants. They multiplied year by year and the General's friends had great sport at the winter shoots.

Tom Samson's hill below and on his boundary was not divided from the Blackberry Hill, unlike most of the Hill inclosures which were partitioned by stone walls. The boundary between Tom Samson's field and the General's was marked by a hedgerow. It is true a lot of the bushes were hawthorn, but here and there a holly bush with dark green spiky leaves and winter berries provided a pleasing contrast to the dormant hawthorn in winter. Furthermore, a giant hollow oak tree in the hedgerow was home for a colony of bees. They had been there for many years and villagers in protective clothing always robbed them of some of the honey. By the gate where the bridle path gave access, an old gnarled apple tree known by the village folk as a Drunken Willie still bore fruit. The hedgerow belonged to Tom Samson.

There was a bit of the Hill near the wood, as Alf Bullen often said, "not worth a hat full of crabs". One might wonder how such a saying originated, eighty miles from the sea, but crabs was the local word for lice.

It was a bitter March day when Alf Bullen said he hated that skinny wind from Russia. He had been helping Evan with the lambing. On the Hill land the flock of Kerry Hill ewes had escaped much of that liver disease called Fluke whereas the Vale men had lost many of their ewes. James Bullen, still agile in his seventies, led the foremost horse with a two-horse team pulling a nine-furrow drill as he and Gilbert planted barley on the flat land above Park Farm. The pheasant shoot being over, David Hicks was busy ridding the wood and the meadow, where he reared his birds, of predators, stoats, weasels, jays.

That morning in March, David was walking the boundary of Tear Coat, part of Tom's estate where David snared rabbits. He was not a man to be easily surprised by things, natural or otherwise, but what he saw did leave him gasping for a while. There had been a very big landslide, which had left a gaping chasm of a trench three feet deep on the Hill.

The hawthorn hedgerow separating the Blackberry Hill from Tear Coat had moved five yards down the hill leaving a big ditch on the General's side of the boundary. The fissure was twenty yards long, and had taken a couple of holly bushes and the Drunken Willie apple tree with it. Luckily the hollow oak tree farther along the hedge remained unmoved.

David Hicks sat on a fallen log, lit his pipe and wondered. He smiled to himself when it dawned on him that his Gaffer, Tom Samson, may have lost five yards of land to the General. Still, he thought, the boundary fence could be put back in its original place, but what of the three-foot ditch where the land had slipped from?

David realised he had to tell Tom Samson and he walked through the woods towards Sheldon to do so. On the way he met Sep Sands coming from Sunshine Farm. David and Sep never had much to do with each other. The gamekeeper was forced to close his eyes to Sep's poaching, knowing, as he did, that Sep was the illegitimate son of Tom. That morning David told Sep he had heard the rumblings of the earth moving during the night. A sound, he said, like distant thunder.

Tom and Sarah Samson, with their daughter, were not surprised by the landslide for such a thing had happened by the Banbury Stone in the last century when a lady riding her horse nearly lost her life and the horse's, and of course Ruth, who studied history, spoke of the underground granary which was exposed there, and the parched wheat.

As soon as the Bullens heard of the landslide in Tear Coat they were there after work, marvelling at the ways of nature and fearful of what they saw. "'Tis known as an act of God," Joe Badger said later at the Cider Mill.

"No," Alfred said, "'tis the Devil. He is responsible for such things. I be mortal afraid of what comes next as our cottage is on the edge of the Hill nearly a thousand feet above the Vale below."

Next day in the sheep fold at Park Farm, Evan Pritchard said he was tired of Alfred's prophecy of doom, and Gilbert, in the barley field, had the same problems with James. At times like this all the legend, the folklore and the ghost-like stories surfaced in the Bullen household.

On the Sunday morning after breakfast, Ruth went to Cobblers Quar to try to explain how the earth moved when the molten heat of the centre cooled. "We are lucky here, compared with America where great earthquakes happen."

Sunday evening at Netherstone Church, Revd Cuthbert met his little flock, some of whom were still concerned about the landslide. Alfred and James sat in their usual pew towards the vestry. They were a good example of the early twentieth-century farm labourer. They wore what was almost a uniform for Sundays, a day when the only work done was tending to the animals. Alfred was smart in his grey fustian suit with cloth-covered buttons, a high waistcoat and starched shirt fronts. The hobnailed boots of working days had been swapped for light, black boots that he called his tea-drinkers. James was dressed identically, apart from his hat. His brother wore a box hat, a cross between a top hat and a bowler; James had acquired a genuine grey trilby, one discarded by Tom Samson that had found its way to a jumble sale.

For some years Joe Badger's wife had done the Bullens' washing, a job her late mother had done. Revd Cuthbert was now aged and very lame. Bertha Brown, who had been housekeeper to the Brice's, was the maid of all work at the Vicarage.

Evensong at Netherstone Church had taken place unaltered for many years, apart from the coming of the Pritchard family, who were quite accomplished musicians. Gwen played the organ and her husband and sons gave extra strength to the choir of half a dozen voices. Ruth Samson was a member of the choir too, along with Jane Hicks. Jane was now engaged to Gilbert Pritchard.

Ruth had spoken to Revd Cuthbert over an afternoon cup of tea at the Vicarage, telling him of how the Bullens and other members of the congregation were upset over the landslide. "It is hard to convince these simple folk that the movement of the earth at Tear Coat was a natural thing. Their belief in a God who is angry and in the power of evil spirits is so deep rooted," she explained.

Revd Cuthbert had been a country parson for so long that he understood. That evening the choir sang "The Church's One Foundation", a sort of affirmation that all was well and the beginning of an evensong of hope for the folk of Netherstone.

In his sermon, the Vicar took for his text "As long as the earth remaineth, seedtime and harvest shall not cease". He did his best to explain that weather conditions were the reason for the landslide. "We have had a hard winter, which is now followed by a dry, cold March. The land at Tear Coat is locally known as Fox Earth Land. It is not stable like the clay of the Vale. When this rather frightening thing is described as "An Act of God", that's purely legal language which exempts landowners from claiming compensation from their neighbours for damage to property. I have seen the gaping trench on the

Blackberry Hill. David Hicks took me there in Mr Samson's dog cart. It is quite spectacular, and I was persuaded to take a photograph."

The feeling of the parishioners after the service was one of relief. The Bullens never would understand, neither did Jarvie Ricketts or Jack Lampit, but at least they had faith in their Parson.

Evensong was at six o'clock that Sunday, late in March. Sep Sands never attended Church but took advantage, while the village worshipped, to poach in the woods. As the cock pheasants roosted in the larches and the beeches of Netherstone Wood, Sep waited as the day moved towards its close. He carried a single-barrel 410 folding gun under his heavy winter jacket, a gun that made little noise. Standing for a few minutes, a cock pheasant made a vertical take-off, perching on the outside branch of a larch tree. Sep took his folded gun from under his coat, took a cartridge from his pocket and fired. Unbeknown to Sep, Sergeant Rook from the next village was meeting the Netherstone police constable on the parish boundary. The pleasant evening had tempted him to take the footpath through Netherstone Wood. He saw Sep standing amid the trees and watched him load his gun and shoot the bird.

Now casually, the Sergeant walked up to Sep as the cock pheasant was being placed in the poacher's pocket. "You brought that one down nicely. Your name is Sep Sands, I believe."

"Yes. What of it?" Sep replied.

"Well, I shall have to charge you on at least two counts. First, shooting game out of season — it ended on

February first. And second, shooting a pheasant on a Sunday. Oh, and have you got a game licence?"

Sep took a gun licence from his inside pocket and showed it to the Sergeant. "That's an ordinary gun licence; it does not include shooting game."

Sergeant Rooks's notebook recorded three charges against Sep Sands:

1) Shooting Game out of season.
2) Shooting Game without a Game Licence.
3) Shooting Game on a Sunday.

Sep stood there alongside Sergeant Rook as day turned into night. He said nothing, until finally he remarked, "What's wrong with shooting game on a Sunday? While it's a protection for the landlords, there's nothing in the Bible against it."

"That's the Law," the Sergeant replied. "And you will hear from the Clerk to the Petty Sessions."

Later, the Court fined Sep £10, or a month in jail. Poor Daisy Sands was so upset. She went to Sheldon from Sunshine Farm and apologised to Tom Samson on her son's behalf. Tom, now a rich man, Master of Foxhounds and a landowner, said to Daisy, "Don't be upset. We know the problem with your son." Then, he took £10 from his pocket and gave it to the one he had romped with in the hay all those years ago.

So, Sep was saved from a month in jail, for where would he have found £10? He used the Cider Mill as his bank, but Joe Badger gave no interest, just pints and pints of cider.

CHAPTER
FIFTEEN

The Shepherd Leaves the Fold

Then the lambing ended at Park Farm in March, each sheep had averaged a lamb and a half. There were, as Alf Bullen said, "half a dozen late lambs to come" which he called Cuckoo Lambs, born when the cuckoo calls over the Bredon Hill.

Alf had suffered that spring from the ravages of time. "'Tis me water works," he used to tell the young shepherd Evan, who gathered agrimony off the Hill to help the old man's complaint.

Alf arrived back at Cobblers Quar on the Friday evening after collecting his pay packet from Ruth at Sheldon. Ruth had been worried. "Alf seems a bit vague, Dad," she had said after he had received his wages.

That night Alfred woke his brother at midnight saying that there were wolves among the sheep at Park Farm. "Nothing of the kind," James retorted. "I can hear a dog fox down by Benedict's Pool, that's all."

"It's wolves, James, and I be gwain to see."

James had difficulty in keeping his brother from going out that night and the next day persuaded him to stay in bed. The Vicar came to see him and prayed for him.

"The wolves will have our ewes and lambs I'm sure, Vicar. They prowls these hills." Alf was still concerned.

Revd Cuthbert smiled patiently and recalled how long it was since wolves were in Britain. Meanwhile, Doctor Overthrow was riding his horse from his Regency house in Netherstone towards Cobblers Quar. The message that Alfred was ill had arrived early that March morning. In a barn quite near the Bullens' cottage, the Doctor knew that he could tie his horse to the manger and give it some hay. It was mid-day. Before seeing Alfred, though, the Doctor had other business to attend to. He had an agreement with Tom Samson that allowed him to shoot over Tom's land, and the Doctor had brought his gun and cartridges with him in his Gladstone bag.

The field where Gilbert Pritchard had planted the barley was grey with pigeons. The Doctor crept up to a spinney where a group of larches sheltered him from view. March is a hungry month for animals and birds, the piercing wind dries all foliage and very little green is to be seen. Now, the Doctor hadn't won cups for shooting at Bisley without being a special marksman. The pigeons, hungry for the barley, were settled only twenty yards from the Doctor's gun. It is true he only carried a folding double-barrel 410 about with the long cartridge, but he had the birds in range. He carefully picked off two birds at the outside of the group. Two pigeons, known as quice or wood pigeon, lay still on the headland. One of the beauties of the 410 was that it gave little noise. All the same, the flock of wood pigeons fled towards the Great Hill Barn by circling the barley field before landing again within range of the Doctor's gun.

Two carefully aimed shots left a couple more of the birds on the headland for the Doctor to pick up.

The Doctor took the result of his little relaxation to the barn where Lavender, his horse, awaited him. The saddle-bag held his gun and the birds. The Doctor strapped the Gladstone bag to the front of his saddle. He mounted and was soon at Cobblers Quar.

"I thought you were never coming, Doctor," James called from the garden gate.

Doctor Overthrow stroked his tidy King Edward VII type beard, replying, "How is Alf? I knew he'd keep for me, and here's some pigeons for a pie."

"Come on in, Doctor. Alf's very muddled, talking of wolves among the sheep."

Alfred Bullen lay on a sofa in the living-room. His first words, as he saw the Doctor prop his gun in the corner of the room, were, "You yunt come to shoot me, Doctor? Don't thee send me to the Workus Infirmary. You know what I hear happens in that place."

"Kind people, Alfred, I'm sure. You do need looking after, but what happens there that you are wary of?"

"Jack be Nimble told me that it was the honest truth. The nurses have a knack of whipping the pillows from under yer head and breaks your neck as short as a carrot. And don't forget, Doctor, I don't want a pauper's grave. There's a stocking with a tidy bit of money under the stairs to bury me."

"Come, come, Alfred. You're not dead yet. You may see another Christmas day or two."

"You see, Doctor, I don't trust the authorities. Take Lofty, for instance, when he came back from Northleach

Jail. They put him on the treadmill and I met him on his return. He was gone to a shadow."

In the walled-in garden Alf's early potatoes were just showing through, tender leaves of a pale green. The buds on the plum trees were bursting into blossom, the bees made music on the blackthorn blossom. The spring of that year looked like being the fall, as the Americans call autumn, for Alfred was too much for James to nurse. Jack Ford took him to Evesholme Infirmary in the dog cart with Ruth Samson sitting by his side.

The ward with old men on iron bedsteads was Alfred's first experience of hospital life. He settled and ate his tea and when the lights went out at eight o'clock he was soon asleep. But Alfred was not at the Infirmary; he dreamed of Bredon Hill and the Cotswold ewes he shepherded before the Pritchards came. "They are through the fence," he shouted at midnight. "Get round 'em, Rosie. Ho, ho, ho. Come on, through the gate." This went on for hours. Men were awake and the male nurse who walked the ward at night woke Alfred.

"Can't you sleep?" he asked.

"Yes, but it's the wolves among my ewes." The candle shone on Alfred's face and he held onto his pillows. "They won't break my neck, surely," he thought.

The next night Alfred was moved to a little ward on his own where he could call the sheep, call his dog Rosie, and hear the wolves howl to his heart's content.

Ruth and her mother, Sarah Samson, went to Cobblers Quar to make supper for James. They feared that he would not cope alone. Gwen Pritchard offered to have him at Park Farm and James was delighted with the move.

The following week Alfred Bullen died aged eighty-four, and James was particular in putting some sheep's wool under his chin before the coffin was screwed down. "This old custom, Vicar," he told Revd Cuthbert before the funeral, "it's an excuse every shepherd should have for not attending church regularly cos of the shepherding."

By now, Ruth Samson and Henry Fairfax from Avon Marsh were what is known as going steady. When Alf died, Ruth said to Henry, "Do you remember when the fox went into the earth by the Banbury Stone?"

"I'll never forget it, Ruth. It was the first time I had seen your charming face. But what of it?"

"The huntsman made the call on the hunting horn 'Gone to Ground'."

"Yes," Henry said but wondered why.

"It's like this, Dear. You know how Alfred has always been so supportive of the Hunt, in fact there were times when he helped Jarvie with the earth stopping. Could you give the hunting call over Alfred's grave at his funeral, 'Gone to Ground'?"

"Of course, Darling," agreed Henry. "Anything to please the good folk of Bredon Hill."

At the Netherstone Churchyard that afternoon in spring the music of the hunting horn with "Gone to Ground" was more meaningful than a half-muffled peal on the bells. A simple man was buried and Netherstone was a little poorer.

James Bullen settled well at Park Farm and Gwen Pritchard looked after him as if he was her father. Up at Cobblers Quar Ruth and Gwen cleaned the place up, and

Gwen was pleased to have some of the furniture from the cottage, paying James for the items. In fact, it was a comfort to the carter, now partly retired, to see some of his bits and pieces around him, especially the Welsh dresser, which had belonged to his mother. At Park Farm it became the pride and joy of the Pritchard family. Never since James' mother's time had it been so polished and shiny in the evening sun. Sitting by the fireside, James felt that he had friends in the Pritchards and the company of something that had belonged to his mother.

Tom Samson knew that James Bullen was not the man he was when he ploughed the fields on Bredon Hill, but he was still found jobs on the farm. When haymaking came, for example, all the men who worked for Tom found their place in a team. Gilbert did the mowing with the two-horse machine. His father built the ricks with Evan and Jack Ford. It was all hands to the pump when the pink-flowered sainfoin bloomed until the ricks were built and thatched. Ruth took her turn with a cob pulling the swath turner, and Jack Lampit loaded the wagons from the pitchers, Gilbert and Evan.

As the two young horses moved between the rows of hay rows, or walleys, James led the filler in the shafts, with a leading rein on the trace horse, still remembering to call "Hold tight" before the team moved on. James called loudly for Jack Lampit to steady himself on the load. It was such a joy for the old carter to be involved in the haymaking. Gilbert had schooled the young horses, and James lovingly fed them from the new-made hay when the wagon stood still. Captain and Colonel, now the retired geldings, grazed in a field over the Cotswold-type wall. "Like me they be," James thought, "long in the tooth."

Tom Samson helped when the rick needed a man on the pitch pole to pass the hay to the rick builders from the half-way stage. He had ridden over from Sheldon and called Owen Pritchard aside as the men had their morning bait. In a low voice he said, "Don't let Jack Lampit have too much cider. We don't want him falling from the load." Owen Pritchard, in his quiet way, was unofficial foreman over the men. He knew what had happened at Sunshine Farm when Jack had sucked cider through a straw.

When there was nothing for James to do on the farm, when the rain held up the work in the fields, he pottered off to Jarvie Rickett's cottage half a mile away. The two men relived the life on Bredon Hill when Queen Victoria's Jubilee meant a bonfire by Parson's Folly. Sometimes Joe the Hermit joined them over bread and cheese and cider. Visits to Jarvie were frequent. Ada, Jarvie's tight-lipped wife, always gave James a welcome. Who knew more about the old gamekeeper than Ada did? "Be Gilbert and Jane still engaged, James?" she asked one day.

"As far as I know, and no doubt there will be a wedding before long."

Jarvie smiled and Ada gave him a look knowing how the old gamekeeper liked to gossip. "There be bundling in bed so I'm told," Jarvie added. "'Tis an old Welsh custom. Nothing like that happened in our day, did it Ada?"

Little did Jarvie know how much Ada had heard about the woman in red at the Castle. Now she raised her voice. "You know, James, my man's got no room to talk seeing what went on with that woman at the Castle. Gilbert and Jane are engaged and what happens on Saturday nights at Camp Cottage is their business, and whatever you think 'tis better than risking bastard kids."

While folks may have gossiped about Gilbert and Jane, no one knew that the engaged couple had their eyes on Cobblers Quar. On Sunday afternoons that year they walked up through the woods to the cottage. Jane had the key. The cottage lay empty now, the rooms smelt damp.

"Will you marry me soon?" These words of Gilbert's came as a start to Jane, but they were words she had wanted to hear. In the curtainless empty place she threw her arms around Gilbert saying, "Of course, but where shall we live?"

"But this place is just waiting for us, Jane. It needs some work done, I know, but Mr Samson is willing to do it up for us."

"Oh, Gilbert! That's all I want, a cottage up here overlooking Netherstone."

"You know Jack be Nimble, the so-called rough carpenter? He has already been asked to make a new staircase, but I'm sure Mr Samson will make this into a little love nest."

Weeks went by, then months, and at last the cottage was perfect. Revd Cuthbert read out the banns in Netherstone Church, one week, the next week, and then a third and final time. A simple wedding, with a breakfast at Park

Farm, then a week's honeymoon to see relatives on the Brecon Beacons, and Jane became one of the Pritchards, living with her husband Gilbert at Cobblers Quar.

"No need for bundling stockings now, James," Jarvie said in his wicked way in front of Ada, who was not amused.

After the wedding and the furnishing of Cobblers Quar Gwen Pritchard asked James, as they sat by the fireside at Park Farm, "Would you mind very much if I gave the Welsh dresser to Jane and Gilbert?"

James shook his head and replied, "What a lovely thought. It's going back to Cobblers Quar, where it belongs."

CHAPTER
SIXTEEN

The Hiring Fair

Stratford Mop or Bull Roast had been the venue for many years where young men, labourers of the farms, were hired by their masters. The length of hire was usually for six years, from Michaelmas to Michaelmas. James Bullen had been hired as a carter when but a boy chap, as he called himself. His employer was a hard man and young James's breakfast had consisted of cider sop, and his sleeping quarters an attic in the farmhouse. He wasn't allowed a candle to light him to bed for fear of fire. Often James looked back on those hard times when he visited Jarvie and Ada, but things began to change for the better after the first seven years of the twentieth century.

"'Tis Stratford Mop next week-end," James announced one evening over supper at Owen Pritchard's house.

"Yes," Owen replied, "and our Evan, the young fool, is going there on Saturday with Jack Ford and Sep Sands."

James remembered those mop fairs before the old Queen's death, and said how every year he bought a pair of strong hobnailed boots that day from his harvest money, boots to keep his feet dry during the winter months.

The trip to Stratford Mop was advertised as an excursion from the local railway stations. Going from Netherstone on the old Midland line meant changing trains at Evesholme station onto the Great Western line. The train left Netherstone station at two o'clock. Dressed in their best corduroys and moleskins, with their boots blacked, Evan, Jack and Sep boarded the train.

Stratford, when the sun went down, was a blaze of light. Up and down the street, bullocks and pigs were being roasted on spits over open fires. Men queued up to buy a good slice of roast beef or pork, sandwiched between the top of a cottage loaf, for just a few pence. The Bredon Hill party feasted with hundreds of fair-goers. They drank the famous local beer. This was an annual holiday to remember.

Evan was interested in the big steam engines tucked away in the side street, engines that provided power for the side-shows of the Mop. Their gleaming brass, the smell of the steam, was intoxicating and, mixed with the beer, gave the men that extra self-importance and confidence. One tent had a notice: COME AND SEE A HORSE WITH HIS TAIL WHERE HIS HEAD OUGHT TO BE. Those men of Bredon Hill paid their pennies to see a horse with his tail in the manger and his head facing them.

One chap was putting watches into envelopes and mixing the packets up on a table. His offer of "Pay me a shilling for a packet" tempted Sep to hand over the money. He opened the envelope to find inside a tie pin and two collar studs. And so the evening went on, with more coppers spent to see the Fat Lady, a nineteen-year-old who weighed over twenty stone. "It's a fake," Sep said and was overheard by the lady on show.

"Touch me then," she said. "I'll prove it."

Gingerly Sep felt the flesh on the Fat Lady's forearms and blushed crimson. "Mind what you be saying," Evan warned the poacher from Sunshine Farm after that.

"Walk up. Walk up. I'll take on all-comers for three rounds in the ring. If you win, the prize is £5, all for half a crown." The old bruiser stood in his pantaloons, his bare chest partly covered by a gaudy red dressing-gown. It was Lud Abello of Spain. Jack Ford turned to his friends and said, "My God! He's had some hammering in his time." And he had indeed. Lud Abello had what is known as a cauliflower ear and a broken nose among his battle scars.

A young farmer chap stepped into the roped-off ring and challenged the old campaigner. The chap seemed quite handy with his gloved fists for the first round. Lud led him on until in the third round a blow to his solar plexus put the farm chap on the canvas floor. Sep noticed that he fell forward to the floor and Jack Ford explained that a blow just above the ribs would paralyse a chap for a while.

Jack Ford took a long look at the coloured picture of a semi-naked lady outside a tent. A sixpence entry fee brought a line of fair-happy, not to mention cider-happy chaps to the tent. When the tent was almost full a woman flaunted her half-naked body in front of the stage, with the three men of Bredon Hill standing in the front row.

She took off her spangled jacket and exposed what Sep called her "tits". She mingled with the folk, brushing her body against Jack Ford, who blushed from ear to ear.

"I'm going to show you as low as possible," she said, reciting the words that she said every day in her tawdry profession. "Now I'm showing you as high as possible."

A united clap came from her admirers, then one older farmer shouted from the back, "Now let's see possible."

The three single men wondered about the ways of women. "A beautiful body," Sep remarked as they left the tent, but Jack Ford, who knew more about the ways of show folk, said, "She's more than second hand, I reckon."

A cart horse with five legs drew the crowd, the three Bredon Hill men included. The horse had a growth from one of its hind legs above the fetlock. From here a bone covered with flesh and hair had been skilfully fitted at the end with a little horseshoe. The shoe didn't touch the ground, but the horse had the semblance of a fifth leg.

A Russian band played military music, a contrast from the steam organ whose old tunes blasted away the night. "What time's the train back?" Evan asked Jack Ford, who took out his watch.

"Ten thirty," Jack replied. "But it's eleven o'clock, so we'll have to walk."

"Let's have another then," Sep volunteered. "I got a few half crowns left." And the three men went into the Red Horse and drowned their thoughts of what might happen on their return.

It was midnight when the three men took the road to Evesholme. "'Tis about eighteen miles you know," said one of the friends. The noise of three pairs of hobnailed boots hitting the hard road became slower and slower. The excitement, the drink, now told them one thing — they needed sleep. By the roadside an open cart shed partly filled with straw just invited the men to lie down. "Here we go, chaps," Jack said and the moon shone like a guiding star into their bedroom that night.

Luckily Evan had bought a loaf of bread and a pound of cheese which, like the loaves and fishes in the Bible, catered for a Sunday morning breakfast as daylight came. "I could fancy a cup of tea, chaps," Jack said as he rose from the straw bed. So, Sep opened his frail basket, took out a coconut and pierced the shell with his shut knife, sharing the milk with his mates.

The road to Netherstone seemed long that Sunday morning as Sep made a classic remark as they plodded through Evesholme — "Where do you think of going for a day out next year, you chaps?" There was no answer to that, just the sound of hobnails on a hard road.

Evan arrived at Park Farm as Sunday dinner was on the table. Gwen Pritchard said very little, other than that youth must have its fling. Sep and Jack had expected tongue pie for dinner, but things were different at Sunshine Farm, where Daisy Sands had been so worried about them that she had seen the Vicar at Church and told him her son and lodger had not returned. When the two men did reach home, Daisy had not cooked dinner.

"You'll settle for some cold bacon and cheese and a cup of tea?" she said, partly in anger, partly in relief. Her next question, "Why *did* you miss the excursion train?", received nothing more than a silence from the two tired, footsore young men who had fallen asleep in their chairs.

CHAPTER
SEVENTEEN

A New Vicar For Netherstone

Not since 1888 had there been such snow and ice on Bredon Hill, but now, twenty years later, the snow fell until the gullies on Great Hill were full to the brim. James whiled away the time by the Pritchard's log fire. He dare not risk the short journey to Jarvie's place. By mid-January the Avon River had frozen, bringing out the skaters, and at Evesholme a fire on the river by the ferry cooked a pork pig.

Evan Pritchard had his ewes safely in a meadow at Park Farm. He and Gilbert both skated from Evesholme to Bredon Lock. The heavy frost split great trees in the woods and when the hoar frost came, Benedict's Pool, surrounded by withies that dipped towards the frozen water, looked like fairyland. There was no prospect of fox hunting for those winter months

Sarah Samson was worried about the Vicar, Revd Cuthbert. He had served the Parish well but now was ailing. She went daily to the Vicarage where Bertha Brown was nursing a sick and aged man. His niece came from away, concerned about his condition. Tom

Samson, as Churchwarden, arranged for a Lay Reader to conduct services. The folk of Netherstone were anxious. They were right to be so, for, on Candlemas Day, Revd Cuthbert died. His funeral, conducted by the Rural Dean, was attended by local clergy. Life in the village and on the Hill stood still while men and women paid their respects to a Good Man.

Tom and Sarah Samson, David and Patience Hicks, Owen and Gwen Pritchard, Gilbert Pritchard and his new wife Jane, Frank and Alice Grove of Higford House, Daisy and Sep Sands all attended. Even Jarvie Ricketts and his wife Ada and James Bullen made their way to Church that cold February day, fetched in a pony and trap by Joe Badger from the Cider Mill.

Henry Fairfax of Avon March rode over to meet Ruth at Sheldon on their way to Church. The couple spent weekends at Sheldon where Ruth did the paper work for her dad. She had little time apart from visiting the folk on her father's farm, but things between her and Henry went steadily on. Ruth was still quite young, and engagement and marriage were something anticipated, but not at the moment.

When the weather improved and Evan's ewes started lambing, the big thatched barn where the giant timbers were marked with Roman numerals where the joints met became a nursing home for the newborn lambs. Evan, now without the help of old Alfred, had Tom Samson's help every evening until midnight to allow the young shepherd some sleep before he returned to the fold from his makeshift resting place in a shepherd's hut near the barn.

Despite the hard winter the Kerry ewes lambed an average of one and a half lambs apiece. Gilbert Pritchard had hauled a couple of wagon loads of sainfoin, that holy hay, from the Hill to the bay of the barn. How those ewes relished the sunshine that seemed to come from the dried pink flowers and the leafy fodder.

James was now able to visit Jarvie and Ada, and old Jack Lampit joined them, warming themselves by the fire and with the metheglin, a mead made from James's honey. He kept a string of straw hives up his garden between the fruit trees. He often related the story of selling a zinc bath full of honey to an Evesholme chemist for fourpence a pound.

Among the topics of the gossip at Jarvie's cottage, where his tight-lipped wife sometimes broke up the conversation if she thought imagination had run riot, was who was going to be the new Vicar and where was Bertha Brown going after the furniture sale.

"None of your business," Ada called from her kitchen.

"Bottles of Communion Wine be missing from the vestry, so it's said. And some think Sep Sands has been drinking it."

These words of Jarvie's brought a titter from Jack Lampit, who said, "A bright fella to take Communion, but as you say nothing's proved." And so the mystery remained.

After the sale of the Vicar's furniture the problem of Bertha Brown solved itself when Frank and Alice Grove of Higford House, who now had two children, took her in as housekeeper, maid of all work, and nanny for the

122

children. Frank Grove employed some labourers on his 200 acres, and Alice spent a lot of time in the dairy, butter-making, and with her poultry.

Every Sunday services were held as usual at Netherstone Church after Revd Cuthbert's death. Neighbouring clergy, some retired, came and conducted the Anglican ritual. Strange though but, whether it was respect for the late Revd Cuthbert or curiosity about who was officiating at the Church, the congregation was somewhat larger than when Cuthbert had been the Priest. "'Tis like this," David Hicks said, with no disrespect to their late Vicar. "We did know more or less what he was going to say at services. These men from away do bring something different, away from monotony."

Speculation about the appointment of a Vicar was talked of in the Cider Mill, especially at weekends when James Bullen, Jack Lampit, and Jarvie Ricketts held court. Sep Sands dreaded these Saturday nights when the three old men repeated their tales over and over again.

"I minds the time when Revd Rand come yer back forty years ago. There was a man, mind!" James then told his story of Rand refusing to baptise babies in the village and how the organ was overrun by mice. "And I'll tell thee what, Rand just went through the motions, never visiting the sick, just riding that big black mare of his around the parish."

"What about the state of the Churchyard? Some said 'twas knee high in clocks and thistles."

"So it was, Jarvie, 'cos I took my hay fork and pitched it over the wall into the field where a farmer's cattle grazed. What do you think old Rand said to me? 'You pitch that back into the Churchyard, 'cos that's my freehold'."

Jarvie said, "I remember him when I was in the choir as a boy. He was suspended from office by the Bishop, but he was long-headed, a scholar, and won his appeal at the Court of something or other."

Jack Lampit recalled how the Vicar at that time fell out with the Squire, and how that shouldn't happen in religion but it does. That corrugated iron chapel in the next village where the Wesleyans met used to be bombarded with stones thrown by some of the Church folk.

At closing time at the Cider Mill that Saturday night Sep had drunk so deeply of the cider that Joe Badger took him home to Sunshine Farm in the dog cart, and the three old men with their candle lanterns took the bridle path to Park Farm and Lenchwick Lane.

On another occasion at the Cider Mill, when the old regulars had been mulling over the question of the new Vicar, Joe Badger, the landlord, had a puzzle. Revd Cuthbert had been essentially a Low Churchman and the smell of incense had not perfumed the old church for centuries. But Joe had asked, "How can you tell a Low Churchman from an Anglo-Catholic?" The question mystified his three old customers that Saturday night at the Cider Mill. They had no answer. Then Joe explained that a Low Churchman wore a wide dog collar, a High Churchman wore a narrow one.

Henry Fairfax's visits to Sheldon were now regular at weekends. His farm at Avon March alongside the river the other side of the Hill was still run by his father, but much of the organisation was now shouldered by young Henry. He and Tom Samson had long discussions about the appointment of a new Vicar for Netherstone. One of Henry's brothers had taken Holy Orders but was well established down in the Forest of Dean.

Ruth did so agree with her mother that the village needed a younger man, one who played cricket and arranged concerts and was able to get around the Hill. The late Revd Cuthbert had been restricted by infirmity for some time.

The empty Vicarage took on a ghostly feel and appearance after Cuthbert's time. The hollow walls rattled with the sound of rats as they took their tunnels through the house. The Pritchard family kept an eye on the place and Evan mowed the Churchyard, but everyone longed for a new man to be their Priest.

At long last a Vicar for Netherstone was chosen and George Mellor came from Oxfordshire, where he had been a curate. George had good references and had an MA from Oxford University.

The Vicarage was quite big for a single man of thirty-two. Patience Hicks, the gamekeeper's wife from Camp Cottage, agreed to be a kind of cook-housekeeper, coming each morning at eight o'clock and finishing at five in the evening. It was understood by the Parochial Church Council that George Mellor would bring his maid with him from Oxfordshire, a girl of twenty named Hannah Loosestrife.

The group who now discussed these things around Jarvie Ricketts's fireside, supping homemade wine, were Jarvie, Jack Lampit, Queenie White, old James Bullen and Ada Ricketts. To say they gossiped would be an understatement.

"What dust think of the Parson's maid?" Jack Lampit said with a chuckle and a wicked look in his eye.

"A tidy body, no more," Ada replied. "Give the girl a chance, they only arrived last week," she added.

Jarvie smacked his mouth, puffed little eddies of smoke from his clay pipe up the chimney, then remarked, "Hair as black as a ravens wing." He followed that by placing a hand on each side of his chest and saying, "What a pair, a wench who could give a gallon of milk a day." Ada and Queenie's remonstrations were drowned by the laughter of Jarvie, Jack and James.

"How many bedrooms are there at the Vicarage?" James said in all innocence as a man who had never been loved by a woman since his mother's death.

"Ah, there's three bedrooms but I recollect that one's anant the other, and there's a doorway in between."

Queenie was emphatic that men of the cloth were different in their morals from her Jack and Ada's Jarvie. "That's just where you be wrong, Queenie. Parsons does no manual work and they be more likely to take advantage of a girl than me or Jack."

James was amused but knew little of the ways of a man and a maid.

"Tell you what," Jack suggested. "If there was a fire the Parson would come out of the same bedroom window as his maid."

The thoughts and words going on around the fire at Alstone Cottage, Jarvie's home, never occurred to the

Welshman Owen Pritchard, his wife Gwen, and Evan the shepherd, at Park Farm. And over at Cobblers Quar Gilbert and Jane were laying the foundations for a good marriage. Gilbert took a pride in the garden, Jane worked with needle and crochet hook in the evenings and helped with the hayfield and harvest in season.

CHAPTER
EIGHTEEN

Sep Sands, Handyman?

Life at Netherstone would never be the same with the new Vicar, George Mellor. He mixed well with the agricultural community, spending Saturday evenings at the Cider Mill and at whist drives in the Reading Room. He was, it must be said, essentially a student of theology, a man of books. His tender, lily-white hands had never done gardening, cut logs for the fire, in fact George needed help and quickly.

Sep Sands, that mystery man of the Hill, did little but prop up Joe Badger's bar at the Cider Mill. When offered a job at the Vicarage doing the small garden, chopping wood and bringing in the coal he agreed at a price. Sep always worked at a price.

Soon Sep was a part of the little staff at the Vicarage. He proved a useful general dogsbody, mowing the lawns, clipping the yew hedge, sawing logs for the big open fire. As Jarvie said, "He will never die of overwork."

It is true Hannah Loosestrife, the Vicar's maid, would have been an attraction to lots of young men of Sep's age, and he was envious in a way of the Vicar. But cider-sodden Sep looked upon women as a different species who did housework, cleaned floors, and decorated their hats.

Long hours on dark nights with the long rabbit net on Bredon Hill or shooting the odd pheasant, poaching, selling his illicit produce to Evesholme, that was Sep's whole life.

He was a man no one ever knew where to find. A stalker of game, a petty thief of fruit, wheeling and dealing in most things that might bring in a few shillings. He thought of those who indulged in sex as being effeminate. Sep was no pervert, he was one on his own. And he was quite unable to understand the ways of women.

The two bedrooms with a door in between were next to the third room, which was smaller and used as a box-room. It was here that Sep stored the apples on sheets of newspaper — the cookers on one side of the room, the eating apples in the opposite corner. Hannah's bedroom was supposedly the middle room between the Master Bedroom and the box-room.

From the landing Sep took his hampers of apples to the box-room for storage. One morning, quite early, Sep noticed that Hannah's bed was unoccupied. She was probably away for the weekend but curiosity got the better of him. The bed was unmade and through a small hole in the timber partition between Hannah's room and the Vicar's, Sep spied two bodies asleep in one bed. Sep, not usually a secretive man, kept this to himself for a while. He was questioned at the Cider Mill but Sep was loyal to the Vicar. Yet that devious chap had ways of revenge. Perhaps Hannah would be a partner for Sep!

At Stratford Mop Fair Sep Sands did his usual rounds of drinking, and visiting coconut shies and side-shows. At one stall a gypsy woman who told fortunes had a display of grotesque masks. One was a representation of the Devil, Old Pecked Ears. The mask, in papier mâché and fixed to the face by elastic bands, was truly frightening, a scaly face with long teeth-like fangs and a red nose between two piercing black eyes. Sep bought the mask and bided his time. Hallowe'en was the following week when the spirits, evil and good, take over as October turns to November.

When Hallowe'en came it was a dark night, a silent night apart from the hooting of the tawny owl and the distant call of a weaned calf from Park Farm. Sep followed the footpath across the walled fields that divided Sunshine Farm from Netherstone and the Vicarage. He carried in his frail basket a large mangel wurzel from which, that afternoon, he had scooped the middle until the root was completely hollow. Two eyes and a nose were carefully cut into the skin of the mangel with a cut below for a mouth.

In the stable at Sunshine Farm in the light of the Hallowe'en afternoon, Sep had fitted the gruesome mask of the Devil on the face of the mangel and had put half a candle inside. The top of the root fitted where the leaves had been trimmed, allowing access for the candle to be lit. Even in the stable at Sunshine Farm during the light of the afternoon the sight of that devilish mask gave a creepy feeling to young Sep. "Wait until dark," he thought. "That's going on a broomstick in the Vestry."

"It's late to go to the Cider Mill," Daisy Sands called to her son as he left, candle lantern in hand, at nine thirty that evening.

"All right, Mother. I may be late back, you know I stay with Joe Badger after closing time."

Sep was just in time for a drink at the Cider Mill, then Joe invited him into the kitchen. "How's Hannah?" he enquired, a bit envious.

"Oh, her's all right. Looks after the Vicarage well according to Patience Hicks."

"Ah," Joe replied. "And does the Vicar look after her?"

"I don't interferc, but I could tell you a lot . . . But I remember I must carry some more logs into the back kitchen."

It was a quarter to twelve when Sep took the logs into the outhouse. One candle burned in the Vicar's bedroom. All was quiet.

At twelve o'clock Sep lit the candle in the mangel with the Devil's mask. He smiled as the face of Old Pecked Ears partly illuminated the Vestry.

The surplices of the choir hung on the wall. Sep carefully wrapped a surplice around the broomstick below the masked figure. The light of the candle shone through the eyes, the nose, the mouth of the mask. Even Sep felt spooked as he tiptoed to the belfry. "I'll ring the funeral bell," he thought, and soon the doleful sound of death stole over the quietness of the countryside. Boom, Boom, Boom, went the bell.

George Mellor sprang from his bed. Hannah called out, "George, what's wrong?" as the Vicar pulled an overcoat over his nightshirt, and in his slippers rushed to the Church.

By now the ringing had stopped, but in the Vestry! George called out, "Beelzebub!" Then he shouted for Hannah to join him.

Hannah ran across the lawn from the Vicarage to the Church shouting, "George, it's Hallowe'en. It's Hallowe'en." Then as she arrived they collapsed together on the Parish Chest and held each other until Hannah plucked up courage to blow out the candle in the mangel wurzel.

"I wonder," the Vicar said, "who played that trick?"

"Sep Sands," Hannah replied. "Sep Sands."

In the morning Sep was working in the vegetable garden of the Vicarage. How was he going to explain last night away?

"Sep," the Vicar said a little angrily, "you played that trick with the Devilish lantern, and you tolled the Funeral Bell."

"Yes, I did," Sep replied without hesitation.

"I shall have to report it to the Parochial Church Council," George Mellor replied.

But Sep held the trump card, saying, "That's all right, Vicar, then I shall tell them that you sleep some nights with Hannah."

"Prove it, Sep, just prove it."

Sep replied, "There's a hole in the wooden partition where a knot has come out. I saw you cuddled up with your maid early one morning."

George Mellor took Sep by the hand and said earnestly, "Don't say a word and I won't."

* * *

Life at the Vicarage was a series of dramas. Sep, it is true, kept the garden in good shape but, as Old Jarvie Ricketts, said, "There's more in that young fella's yud than the comb ull take out."

Sep trapped badgers and sold the skins in Evesholme with the rabbits he had caught and the poached pheasants. Daisy, his mother, never knew when he would be home at Sunshine Farm. Sarah Samson often chided her husband about the liberty he allowed Sep, but Tom just brushed it off.

The fact was that Sep had been devious yet diplomatic in not telling all and sundry that Tom was his father and making play of the incident in the hayfield when Tom had lain with Daisy, the genesis of his birth. Remember that Sep had seen relations between George Mellor, the young Vicar, and his maid, Hannah Loosestrife. He was too fly to let on but he did so at a price, for instance the Hallowe'en Funeral Bell and the image of the Devil in the Vestry.

George Mellor was a generous man, a man of the people, and often on winter nights he invited David and Patience Hicks to the Vicarage to sit by the fireside with Sep Sands. Hannah Loosestrife served the drinks, cool from the cellar.

One surmises that the morning Sep peeped through the knot hole and saw the Vicar in bed with his maid was no more than a kiss and a cuddle.

CHAPTER
NINETEEN

Owen Pritchard's Goose

Things between the Vicar and his maid may have stayed as innocent as a kiss and a cuddle had it not been for the happenings on one moonlit night when Hannah was on her way home after an evening with Bertha Brown, housekeeper and nanny at Higford House. She walked past Camp Cottage, past Queenie White's place in Lenchwick Lane, taking the footpath to the Vicarage. It was half-past ten and the moon made shadows over the corn field and played hide and seek with the fir trees on the edge of the Hill. Hannah had been told so many stories about the ghost of Benedict's Pool but the field known as Clay Furlong was some distance from there.

Hannah walked passed the Stone Hill stile and was almost in the Vicarage garden, but in the paddock adjoining she suddenly saw something that night that she would never forget. A pair of white wings flapped and from the object on the footpath a scream came and the great creature's wings were like some angel, good or bad. Hannah's screams echoed around as villagers came to their doors. The Vicar, George Mellor, ran towards Hannah, who was shaking like a leaf. One of Owen Pritchard's geese had been trapped in a rabbit wire set by none other than Sep Sands. As she sobbed with George Mellor's arms around her the two stumbled into the sitting-room.

"Oh, that man!" the Vicar shouted with anger. "I must release that poor bird."

"Don't leave me," Hannah pleaded, and the two retraced their steps to the footpath where Hannah held the goose while the Vicar slipped the wire snare from its neck.

"You need something to revive you, dear Hannah. Our usual Madeira is not strong enough for this occasion." And George Mellor uncorked a bottle of malt whisky.

On the couch at the Vicarage the two, man and maid, lay in each other's arms. As the grandfather clock warned for midnight, Hannah said, "Shall we go up the wooden hill together?"

The candle burned on the washstand as the Vicar took off his clerical clothes and Hannah discreetly put on her nightdress behind the side of the wardrobe. "'Tis not right, you know, for a Parson to sleep with a maid," Hannah said haltingly.

"We have our feelings, Hannah. Take Revd Bowler, from the other side of the Hill. He is seen most days on his tricycle and it is parked outside the school mistress's house."

When George Mellor blew out the candle the great full moon made patterns on the wallpaper and images on the counterpane of the double bed. George held Hannah's breasts gently and her sobbing ceased. "He is so gentle," Hannah thought. When the Church clock struck the hour of two Hannah knew that nature had taken its course and she was no longer a virgin.

* * *

There was still much speculation on the sleeping arrangements at the Vicarage. Sep Sands was more than careful what he told the customers at the Cider Mill. Jarvie Ricketts thought that plying young Sep with cider would loosen his tongue and so reveal all.

Among his other pursuits, Sep took over the bar on Mondays to allow Joe Badger a little time off in town. Customers had to put up with cigarette ash in their beer on such evenings. Sep smoked the eternal Woodbine — a chain smoker. Jarvie reckoned that the one match that Sep struck first thing in the morning would last him all day as he lit up one Woodbine from the butt end of another.

So the rumour and speculation was rife in Netherstone. Ruth Samson said on one occasion to Henry Fairfax, "A village Parson is never right for everyone. If he goes to the pub that is wrong with some, and with some men of the cloth in parishes where he has a wife that is something to complain about. You see, Henry, if one can't find fault with the Vicar, then one can always with his wife's hat. It is difficult but, of course, George Mellor is putting himself in some danger living with Hannah Loosestrife."

Patience Hicks, who did for the Vicar, as it is known, washed and ironed on Mondays. At first she washed the sheets off two beds, a fourposter in the Vicar's Master Bedroom, and the sheets off a single bed in Hannah's room. Detective if you like, but Patience noticed that for some weeks only one bed had been occupied, and that the one in the Master Bedroom. Again Patience was not one to spread gossip. She left that to the club of men who met at Jarvie's house, now joined by John Brice.

Sep had remained silent since Hallowe'en, and Patience confided only in David Hicks, her husband. Such men as David, a gamekeeper, keep their own counsel; they listen rather than talk. Time had gone on so quickly since Jane Hicks, their daughter, had married Gilbert Pritchard and made a home at Cobblers Quar. They now had a baby son named Owen, who was a delight to this Welsh family.

By Christmas that year it was evident that Hannah Loosestrife was expecting, too. Jarvie Ricketts said to Jack Lampit at one of their meetings around the fire, where the home-made wine was never rationed, "Young Hannah looks promising."

"What do you mean?" came the retort from Ada.

"Her's in the family way."

Jack Lampit added, "In the family way! Wait till hers as old as me and she ull be in everybody's way."

"'Tis not a joking matter," Queenie White told those old rascals, and she was right.

Just as the new Vicar had brought changes to Netherstone, so there were developments at Sheldon too. Tom Samson had increased his stud of hunters and point-to-point horses. In Jack Ford he had acquired a very capable groom As the mares foaled it was obvious that another hand was needed to train, to school, the stud. Fred Alderton had served in the army during the Boer War. Since then he had had some success at an establishment owned by a trainer of steeple-chasers.

Tom found him a job at the stables and a little cottage, tucked away in Battenswood, for him and his wife.

A spare man of forty-six, who dressed in moleskin trousers and wore a bush man's hat, Fred was certainly a man who added to the already picturesque scene on Bredon Hill. His wife, Cath, and son, Gerald, now fourteen, had come with Fred from Shropshire.

Things had changed since Tom Samson had depended on Alfred and James to shepherd and plough and do most of the farm work on the Hill. Now Owen Pritchard, as stockman and foreman, had a team that could be relied on. Tom and his wife Sarah had great support from Owen from Park Farm. He ran the farm with great ability, and their daughter Ruth dealt with the clerical side of the enterprise. This allowed Tom Samson to be both Master of the Fox Hounds and now an owner and trainer of racehorses. A modest group of bloodstock, four mares and their foals served by a stallion from down in the Vale, were the nucleus of something that could be an important feature of life on Bredon Hill.

The farmer at Higford House turned his cart horse into the adjoining Spring Hill, Tom Samson's land. One mare, Pleasant, heard the stallion's whinney and strayed into Samson's field. James Bullen said when she foaled in May, a useful colt, after a free service she had "stole the horse". Sunshine Farm, where Daisy Sands had struggled for many years, finally became too much for this elderly widow. Had her son Sep been more helpful, things might have been different. At long last, she sold the land to Tom Samson, who had longed for a racecourse to be developed on Bredon Hill. The racecourse became a venue for point-to-point meetings patronised by the local hunt. Fred Alderton and Jack Ford between them schooled and trained some useful animals for Tom Samson. His ambition was to win at Cheltenham, and after much soul-searching he bought a horse trained on the Hill and won a novice race.

The land at Sunshine Farm lay between two beech woods, a flat plateau of thyme-scented turf over limestone. Daisy kept a paddock for her poultry and still had Jack Ford, the groom, as a lodger.

The racecourse was constructed by Tom's labour force. In fact, the workers who made the jumps from the nearby gorse varied in age from James Bullen, who was now seventy-two, to young Gerald Alderton, a lad of fourteen. Gerald, tutored by his father Fred Alderton, was showing promise over the sticks. The racecourse was a hobby enterprise for Tom Samson. He had no wish to compete with the courses at Cheltenham or Worcester.

Within the family, Ruth's courtship with Henry Fairfax was not the passionate affair expected of young couples in love. They both took life quietly. Henry entertained this attractive young lady at Avon March and he was always welcome at Sheldon. Short leisure times were spent at hunt balls, which were within reach in the Vale and on the Cotswolds. They wined and dined at the best hotels and were regular theatre-goers at Stratford. There was no rush for marriage but the understanding was there and all important. The couple were happy to spend time with one another, and not to rush.

CHAPTER
TWENTY

Christmas to Mothering Sunday

At Christmas Ruth Samson accepted Henry Fairfax's proposal of marriage and an engagement party was arranged at Sheldon. The wedding would probably not be for some time for Tom Samson had suggested to Henry and Ruth that he would convert a stone barn a quarter of a mile away for their first home if that was acceptable. The couple were thrilled by the prospect of living there and being able to control Henry's farm at Avon March. Meanwhile, Tom Samson had plans for Henry to be his partner in the enterprise on the Hill.

Ruth was worried about Hannah's condition — it was now evident that she was expecting. She went over to the Vicarage one day while the Vicar was away. She asked Hannah, "Is it true what we hear — that you are expecting the Vicar's baby?"

Hannah burst into tears. "True, Miss Ruth, too true. It all happened when I saw the goose that night in Sep's rabbit wire. I was frit to death."

"How did it happen, Dear?" Ruth said, lovingly putting her arms around the buxom country girl.

140

"'Twas like this, Miss Ruth, I was sobbing when George half carried me from the paddock. We were used to having what the Vicar called Madeira before bedtime. He's a good man, Miss Ruth."

"Oh, I know he is, Hannah, but I fail to see the connection between the goose in the rabbit wire and you being pregnant."

"Well, Miss Ruth, we drank a bottle of whisky between us, he said to calm my nerves. The grandfather clock I remember warned for twelve o'clock, you know just a few minutes before the hour, and together we went up the wooden hill. I do remember that, and when the candle went out the Vicar held my tits with both hands below the neck of my nightgown. I can't describe the feeling of being cared for, loved I suppose, and after a time we coupled."

Ruth blushed and mopped her brow; she had never been told such a story before.

"Think he will marry me, Miss? I'd like him to."

"I think he ought to, Hannah. You have never been with another man, have you?"

"Oh, no! God's truth I haven't. That was the first time."

That Christmas, as ever, Daisy Sands made a little money from her geese. She dressed them and sent them to market. George Mellor had ordered one for Christmas Day; Sep was supposed to deliver it. He, handy with his gun, had killed pheasants roosting on the fir trees by Cobblers Quar. "Pity to give that goose to the Vicar," he thought as he walked down the Hill to near where Henry Fairfax had his farm at Avon March.

Now, Sep had helped Daisy, his mother, to dress geese for market. In fact, Sep was handy skinning rabbits, badgers, plucking pheasants, anything to make some cider money. One day shortly before Christmas, he was walking with his gun, the folding 410, alongside the River Avon when a swan sailed by with her full-grown cygnets, easy to distinguish by their plumage. He shot one near the bank and pulled the dead bird towards him with a crooked stick — a beautiful bird, quite illegal, the property of King Edward VII, but a trophy for Sep.

When he had plucked and dressed the bird, it was indistinguishable from a gosling. He had a customer at the Cider Mill for the goose his mother had given him for the Vicar. This swan would do for George Mellor. In the Vicarage kitchen on Christmas morning Patience Hicks cooked a bird that she thought was a goose. No one except Sep knew that it had come from near Avon March.

The dinner Patience cooked that Christmas was a great success and the Vicar said that the bird was the best young goose he had tasted!

Sep Sands had little thought for Hannah Loosestrife's condition. Why should he? "That's the Vicar's problem," he thought. But the folk at the little cottages and farms on Netherstone Hill were all wondering what would happen to the poor girl. Only the group of old men at Alstone Cottage where Jarvie Ricketts entertained were more scathing. Jack Lampit referred to Hannah as being "close to profit", while Jarvie's comment was "if you plays with fire you get your hands burnt, and the

Reverend and his maid have no doubt been playing at Mothers and Fathers."

"Such talk," Ada and Queenie White said with one voice.

Patience Hicks, who did for the Vicar, was loyal but concerned about Hannah. Sarah Samson, on a visit to the Vicar, made it known to him that the goings-on could not be tolerated. It was Mothering Sunday the following day and what sort of an example was he, George Mellor, setting for the villagers of Netherstone? "Marry the girl, George. It's the only answer," she said.

The Vicar replied quite curtly, "What! Me with a degree at Oxford marry the daughter of a common workman!"

"You will see, George. Now so many will not take Communion or even go to Evensong. You have made your bed and must lie on it. Good morning to you."

George Mellor, however, had ideas of marrying Hannah to Sep Sands and was bold enough to raise the subject. Sep, the gardener handyman, was cutting the Vicarage lawns for the first time on a spring day. Patience Hicks and Hannah were preparing dinner when George Mellor left his study to see Sep. Their conversation ranged from the blossoming plum trees to the damage done by the wood pigeons to the spring cabbage. Finally, the Vicar got to the real reason for his chat. "You realise that Hannah is, so to speak, expecting a baby in the summer?"

"Yes. I'm not blind to the situation when she passes me by in the hall."

"Don't be so coarse man. This is serious."

Sep replied, "It's your problem not mine."

The Vicar paused a while and then said, "Will you marry Hannah? I'll give you £20 to do so."

"What! £20! I can get more than that for deals at Evesholme and the Cider Mill. You have had the game, now give the baby your name, Sir. I am not looking for a wife and am quite happy living at Sunshine Farm and having a bob or two on Tom Samson's racehorses." And that was the end of that.

One by one, over the next few weeks, the Communicants at Netherstone Church dropped off. Anything that went wrong in the village was attributed to the Almighty's vengeance because of George Mellor's affair with his maid. Liver Fluke among the sheep in the Vale was rife that spring. Evan Pritchard, sent to a farm sale near Evesholme to buy in lamb ewes for Tom Samson, bought thirty from a Vale Farm. They appeared sound in February but by March, when they were due to lamb, the tell-tale signs of a lump under their jaw and a glassiness to their eyes indicated Fluke or Liver Rot.

As they died before they lambed, Evan was distraught, burying the carcasses on the Hill. Then four of Owen Pritchard's Shorthorn cows aborted, and others had a condition then called garget or mastitis.

"The Almighty is warning this Parish of His anger. It happened according to the Bible. Jonah was told to go to Nineveh, so Revd Cuthbert used to say, and I'll go to Hell if he didn't disobey and went to Tarshish. They be places out East I reckon." These words of James Bullen

144

were taken seriously by the group meeting at Alstone Cottage.

"Oi. I remember," Jarvie said. "He was swallowed by a whale. You can't go against The One Above."

CHAPTER
TWENTY-ONE

Easter at Netherstone

Young George Mellor won't get a lot out of the Easter offering," Jarvie said with a chuckle to the wine drinkers of Alstone Cottage.

"Why's that?" Queenie White questioned.

"You should know," Ada spoke for her husband. "Parsons always gets the Easter Offering as a present from the Parish, and it looks as if the congregation will be in penny numbers."

As Easter approached, the subject on the mind of all the parishioners was that of Revd George Mellor's relationship with his maid Hannah Loosestrife. Hannah had insisted that the Vicar was to take her to Benedict's Pool at midnight when the moon was full. She believed the answer to her plight lay in those waters. The event would act as a charm. The Vicar got his orders from the Spirit world, but not without the help of Sep Sands . . .

Full moon was on Saturday night at the end of March, the weekend before Easter. The Vicar had agreed to take Hannah to the Pool. He had invited a few of his Church members to a supper that Saturday night at half past nine. Many refused his invitation. The Pritchard family objected to the Vicar's indiscretion. Tom and Sarah

146

Samson looked on it as a cheek and refused. Ruth, however, did support Hannah and attended the party, while Patience Hicks, the housekeeper, cooked a meal. The old guard of Jarvie, Ada, Jack Lampit, Queenie White, Jim Brice and old James Bullen, all came too.

Sep Sands tapped a barrel of Malvern Hill Perry to serve before the meal. He told Patience Hicks that he had some mushrooms for her to cook with the steak. Sep was not a 1908 drug addict but he knew the effect that the magic mushrooms off the Hill could have, giving hallucinations. Sep did have some feeling for Hannah, it is true, but marriage to her as suggested by the Vicar was out of the question.

Patience Hicks wondered about the mushrooms, fungi Sep had dried and stored for use. She cooked them with the steak and onions after the company had lowered the contents of the barrel of Perry. Sep had a word with Hannah and Ruth, advising them that the mushrooms didn't suit everyone and especially Hannah in her advanced condition.

By eleven that evening, after the meal, Sep said that the party were, as the saying goes, "talking about their Grandfathers". James Bullen recalled the Roman Emperor at the Horse Camps. Revd Mellor said he didn't expect anything like that but the Spirits did appear at the Benedict's Pool, it is said.

It was eleven thirty when the party finished and everyone left the Vicarage and took the bridle path to Benedict's Pool. Even Joe the Hermit at the Folly would never venture there at full moon. The party was buoyed on by the Perry and the mushrooms, all but Sep,

147

Patience, Ruth and Hannah. Ruth and Patience held Hannah's arm all the way to the Pool.

As they approached, the monks at the Monastery below were chanting beautiful music that carried through the crisp night air. Tawny owls answered each other in the woods, "Tu-whit, tu-whoo". An old sow badger was hunting rabbits in the ride. Just a peaceful spring night as the clock at the Monastery struck twelve.

The Pool itself was fuller than usual as heavy rain had flooded the brook. A gaggle of wild geese drifted silently on the water, and the fish, as they rose and fell, made plopping noises in the darkness. The party stood on the edge opposite the tunnel that led to the Castle. A regular thump, as would come from the feet of marching men, came from the tunnel, but in reality was nothing more than a water ram installed by Tom Samson to pump water to the higher fields on the Hill.

Without warning a voice suddenly came from the tunnel, a voice heard only by those who had eaten the magic mushrooms. It was the voice of a woman, who appeared to be a nun, calling, "Your Priest has ravished his maid."

James Bullen said to Jack Lampit, "I'll go to Hell. Did you hear that?"

That moment a figure in white splashed across the water. She screamed, "Marry your maid George Mellor or there's trouble, more trouble. The Roman soldiers are near." All at once, shots were heard in the woods — Sep Sands had fired tracer bullets above the poplar trees.

"On your knees," the voice came from the water, and George Mellor took Hannah's hands.

"Marry me, I love you," he said.

"Three cheers for the Vicar and his maid," someone shouted, bringing a chorus from the party.

Hannah, Ruth, Patience and the Vicar, Revd George Mellor, made their way back to the Vicarage. George, still in a trance from the hallucination he had experienced at the Pool, was supported by Patience Hicks, while Ruth and Hannah lead the way. When they reached the Vicarage Sep met them in the paddock with the pony and dog cart. "Just wondered if you needed a lift," he said with a wry smile."

Concerned about his old parishioners, the Vicar replied, "Quiet Sep. Take the old folk to their homes. They need transport. You will find them near the Pool."

That crisp moonlit night the combination of Perry and mushrooms and what they had imagined (or was it real?) was too much for Jarvie Ricketts, his wife Ada, Jack Lampit and Queenie White, James Bullen and Jim Brice. They stumbled hand in hand to a partly cut hayrick by the footpath. Jarvie had said "We can't stop here by the Pool. I've just seen the Devil pass by, all spiky red hair, with lights shining from his staring eyes. 'Tis an unkid place."

On the sweet smelling hay where Owen Pritchard had left a ridge, the old folk of Netherstone lay silent and fell asleep. When Sep's dog cart came down the track to pick them up the sound of wheels and the jingle of harness woke them. Was this another frightening sign that they were not alone?

"How, how, how. Where are you?" Sep called.

"'Tis that tawny owl," Queenie said as she gripped Jack Lampit's arm.

"I hear wheels," Ada Ricketts shouted. "Is it the Devil? I've seen him and his wicked angels. Hold me tight Jarvie, we will go together."

When Sep pulled up by the hayrick he saw the group in the moonlight, all huddled together, very afraid. "'Tis me," he called from the cart. "Get on board. I'm here to take you home."

As the party reached Alstone Cottage Queenie and Jack Lampit stayed on the cart. "Can't you walk from here to Lenchwick Lane?" Sep questioned.

"No, Sep. I'm petrified, and so is Jack," stuttered Queenie.

Ada Ricketts, not known for giving overnight hospitality at the small Alstone Cottage, put her arm around Queenie saying, "You and Jack can stay here overnight. You too, Jim Brice."

As the Monastery bell struck two o'clock and the distant chanting of the monks came on that clear night, the old parishioners of Netherstone at last felt that some sort of order had returned to the Hill. But sleep was out of the question. Jarvie put some more logs on the fire and Ada made a cup of tea. Round that kitchen table some did nod off, but then came to, still conscious of that frightening midnight at Benedict's Pool.

Back at the Vicarage the Vicar told Patience, Ruth and Hannah he was going to marry his maid. He loved her, he always had.

Henry Fairfax arrived to take Ruth back to Sheldon, where she told her story to the man she loved.

"Marry Hannah! The Vicar? That's wonderful," he said. "And soon *you* will be in my arms for ever as Mrs Fairfax."

No need for a hayrick for Ruth and Henry; they spent the rest of the night on the Chesterfield in the Samsons' drawing-room.

The news of the Vicar's prospective wedding with Hannah Loosestrife spread around Netherstone. James Bullen told all the happenings to the Pritchards at breakfast the following morning. "We did hear the voices and the Vicar responded, and I saw the Devil, an awful experience." Gwen Pritchard smiled as she put the bacon and egg in front of the old man, who continued, "Tell you what, Owen, we may be free from disease in the sheep fold and the cow stalls now his Reverence is doing the right thing. The Almighty will have His way."

On Easter Sunday morning a neighbouring Vicar conducted the service at Netherstone Church. His subject was forgiveness and the reading from the Bible was the woman at the well. She had been unfaithful but would be forgiven.

The banns were read out for the first time of asking, Banns between George Mellor, bachelor, Clerk in Holy Orders, and Hannah Loosestrife, spinster, of Netherstone.

Towards the end of April a quiet wedding was arranged between the Vicar and Hannah. Evan Pritchard was best man, and a niece of the groom acted as bridesmaid. Old Jarvie called it a shot-gun wedding, which was perhaps appropriate in view of the shots from Sep's gun that moonlit night over Benedict's Pool when the flashes had so bemused the party.

151

Time went on and the birth of Hannah's baby was expected early in June. She had a beautiful boy child, who was baptised David Thomas, perhaps a tribute to two of the men on the Hill.

Patience continued as housekeeper but the Vicar was emphatic that Hannah should have a nurse-maid, an educated young lady who would teach Hannah some of the finer points of being the Lady of the Vicarage. Susan Kemp came from an agency and soon the baby thrived. Hannah began to speak in a ladylike manner and learnt from Susan a thing called "etiquette".

Now the Vicar and Hannah had married and their son had been born, Netherstone settled down. It became a close-knit community. It's true Sep Sands, that free spirit of Sunshine Farm, was still a law unto himself — what James Bullen called a Rodney — but he was accepted as such.

That year the farming side of Netherstone proceeded at a pace when Henry Fairfax was made a partner on the Estate. More village boys found work on the Hill and were tutored in cultivation by Gilbert Pritchard, who now ploughed two farms with three horses abreast. Evan showed young men the mystery of shepherding and Owen the milking herd.

The point-to-point course on what was previously Sunshine Farm proved a success. Fred Alderton trained some useful bloodstock while his son, young Gerald, seemed born to the saddle, riding winners on the Hill and around. The hunting season was over, and now Jack Ford, the pioneer of Tom Samson's stable, took second place to Fred Alderton but was nevertheless a useful groom.

For some years Tom Samson and others had let a brookside meadow to the Cricket Club. This land, away from his Estate, flooded in winter but a close-cropped turf made a good wicket for the Netherstone team. On those Saturday mornings Gilbert Pritchard mowed the field using an old nag from the farm. He fitted her with leather shoes over her hooves to prevent any damage to the turf. After a wet, cold winter the summer baked the clay land and by Whitsuntide the cricket pitch was what Old James described as "as hard as the Devil's back teeth".

On Whit Saturday, Netherstone's fixture was home to a team from Evesholme. The Pritchards, Jack Ford, and Henry Fairfax were among the Netherstone team. The Evesholme captain had a particularly fast bowler. Henry Fairfax and Revd George Mellor opened the batting for Netherstone. Those two college-trained players had what is known as style at the wicket. Evan Pritchard came in first wicket down and he was a hard hitter. His strokes could be described as haymakers. He was soon out, caught on the boundary. Jack Ford followed him at the crease.

Jack was very different, a man difficult to get out, a stone-waller who played defensive cricket. One fast ball kept low, but Jack's bat was apparently angled back towards the stumps. The ball, travelling at great pace, bounced from the blade of the bat and hit Jack behind his ear. He fell to the ground like a stone, killed outright on that field by the brook. Netherstone lost a good quiet man, Tom Samson lost a valuable groom and a mother lost a son. Lodging as he had done with Daisy Sands, she had treated him as a son.

A cloud came over the village community. Revd Mellor's awful task was to bury the first young man since he came to the village, and he had been standing at the opposite end of the cricket field from that fast ball.

CHAPTER
TWENTY-TWO

Autumn in Netherstone

After a summer of hot sun, the shirt-sleeved men of Netherstone didn't relish the shortenings days, but autumn came, with a stillness, an oppression that could be felt. And what of the sights and sounds of that season of harvest?

On the Hill the peewits called over their nests, the now rare voice of the corn crake, or land rail, a bird that, on occasions, ran rather than flew in front of the harvesters. The croak of the bird made a noise like striking a comb. The music of the skylark, that high soprano of the air, mingled with the mezzo soprano of the thrush, and after a shower the blackbird sang a deep contralto lullaby at evening. The tawny owl forecast a fine day when it hooted at night-time. The vixen screamed in the woods, a sound like, perhaps, the whetting of a scythe as some smallholder cut his May-sown barley.

The hoar frost gave a fairyland look to the countryside, a gossamer of spiders' webs that the old folk said brought the dreaded husk or hoost to the young cattle as they grazed the frosted grass.

As the nights began to draw in, the cottagers' kettles sang on the hob, logs crackled on the hearth, the yellow glow of the oil lamp cast shadows on the flowered wallpaper as families had their evening meal to the sound of the autumn wind howling down the chimney and the ticking of the long case clock.

Evan Pritchard certainly had a good crop of lambs from the Kerry ewes and, as the Liver Fluke had decimated the flocks in the Vale, good lambs were at a premium.

Alfred Bullen had always driven his flock for sale in Evesholme Market along those six miles of lanes. It was often a long job on warm autumn days to go to the sales. Evan had ideas that Tom Samson found practical. On the Estate they used four-wheeled drays for jobs on the farm, feeding cattle and sheep in winter. Gilbert had three steady half-legged nags all capable of working in the shafts. "If we had some racks on the drays the lambs could go to market in comfort," Evan suggested.

Tom agreed and added, "It would save the hindrance created by any lame animals on the road."

The three drays were fitted with high-sided racks, and each dray was capable of carrying twenty or so lambs. On Market Day at the Evesholme lamb sale Tom Samson's lambs travelled on the drays. Gilbert drove one, Evan another and Owen the third.

James Bullen came to the yard at Park Farm and looked on at this new concept in livestock transport. He pondered and said, "Maybe it's all right but I doubt if brother Alfred would have agreed. He didn't like the Gaffer getting rid of the Cotswold flock." As Old James prodded the lambs through the racks on the dray he said, "How heavy do you reckon these Welsh ship be, Evan?"

Evan answered quickly, with the accent of Brecon, "Oh, these Kerrys are about seventy pounds apiece."

James replied, "Seventy pounds! Alf's Cotswolds were twice that weight."

"Maybe," the shepherd said, "but how long did it take? They were slow developers and the housewife doesn't care for big joints nowadays."

Over at Cobblers Quar Jane Pritchard had a baby girl, the darling of Gilbert's life. His shire mares had foals on the Hill and soon the horse power of the farm would increase. More land was under plough with Gilbert using the three horses on a two-furrow implement, and Owen, after seeing to his cattle, ploughed with two more horses on a single-furrow Ransome plough.

Henry Fairfax's father was ailing and Henry decided to put a bailiff in at Avon March. He was now a partner to his intended father-in-law. He was to marry his daughter, Ruth, in November. The stone barn conversion near Sheldon was complete with all the modern conveniences that were available in 1909. This was going to be the Netherstone wedding of the century.

There was no need really for Ruth to take too much trouble with her appearance, she was so beautiful. Her wedding dress and those of the two bridesmaids, Henry's cousins, came from the premier fashion house in Cheltenham. Henry, all six foot two inches of charm, and his brother, the best man, in their toppers and tails were the main attraction on the men's side.

Revd Mellor conducted a choral service, and all the village seemed to be there, including James Bullen, resting on his ash plant stick. Horses and carriages took the guests to the reception at an Evesholme hotel. The couple were waved off at Evesholme station for London, then to Tilbury where an ocean liner on its way to Italy was their first home.

That evening Tom and Sarah invited villagers to a supper at Sheldon. Netherstone had witnessed a society wedding with guests from some of the most well-known families in Gloucestershire and Worcestershire.

The folk of the village had suffered so much from fantasy and reality, folklore and indiscretions, but as 1910 approached things were looking brighter, and Henry and Ruth were to spend their first Christmas at Prospect House.

Henry and Ruth Fairfax had been married a little over a year when Bredon Hill was scorched by the hottest summer in living memory. The Pritchards at Park Farm had a problem keeping their large herd of cows fed during such a drought. The deep-rooted lucerne in the Vale fields yielded reasonable crops of hay, while the sainfoin on the Hill was a boon. The farmers around Netherstone lopped the brookside withies to give some green fodder for their cattle.

That year the corn harvest was light. Horse beans were popping from their pods in the tropical sunshine. The Pritchards decided to carry the beans and rick them at night when the dew gave some dampness. Tom Samson had never seen the like in his long farming career.

As usual the men had their harvest money when all was safely gathered in. This year they drew their £2 extra wages on August Bank Holiday. James Bullen saw that last harvest through and died there in the rickyard as the last load was pitched from wagon to rick, what Old James had always called "The one the cobbler threw at his wife," i.e. the last.

CHAPTER
TWENTY-THREE

Ayshon's Former Monastery?

Whether the big mansion just above the moat pond at Ayshon was a monastery no one seems to know. The ruins of the building, a hundred yards above the Churchyard, remain today as well as the moat, or fish pond.

Near the Church Fred Alderton's grandfather fought off the Press Gang with his scythe. It was this man who told the story of the mansion to his grandson. Early in the First World War, many men of Bredon Hill had gone into the army. Of those left behind, Jarvie Ricketts often said, "We be the rejects holding the Fort."

Fred Alderton entertained some of his neighbours at the Cider Mill pub — Jack Lampit, Queenie, Jarvie and Ada Ricketts. The pub was a place of refuge for the folk off the Hill, where a good log fire roared up the open chimney on winter nights.

Fred recalled his grandfather's story, that the house was haunted and the last man to live there was Luke Coney, a miser who sold himself to Satan but had to provide for the wants of three witches. He was deserted by his retainers, despite his wealth. His Master, Satan, it is said, threatened to claim him body and soul. Ada Ricketts screamed as Fred told the story, and the storyteller admitted it scared him as a boy.

For a while Luke Coney kept Pecked Ears at bay, imprisoned the witches in a hollow ash tree anant the oak, which still stands near where the mansion was built. He laid a spell, but as Coney ventured from the charmed circle he was seized by the Devil in the haunted mansion, who attempted to carry him up the chimney. The chimney was too narrow and tore him apart, but the Devil took off his scarf, the spell was released, the ash tree split in half and the witches escaped. The remains of the miser lay mutilated on the hearth.

The miser's remains were buried by the Churchyard wall, and his ghost could often be seen searching for his lost soul with terrible groans until the haunted mansion was pulled down. The oak tree still marks the site, but the ghost no longer haunts the spot. Maybe the man was murdered for his hoard of gold, which was never found.

Ruth Fairfax was concerned that Fred Alderton's tales would worry the two old couples of the Hill. Tom Samson's daughter had always been so thoughtful, her beliefs fundamental, and she had always supported the Church and Revd Mellor.

The grass-covered mounds where the house once stood formed a rectangle, in which the grass turned yellow in the hot summer sun. Foundation stones still peep through the surface and the witches' oak awaited the April cuckoo. Maybe Ruth had a great influence on

161

the simple old folk of the Hill and she admitted that things spiritual would never be understood this side of the hereafter. She quoted Wordsworth:

I heard among the solitary hills low breathing coming after me and sounds of indistinguishable steps almost as silent as the turf thus trod.

Those folk, despite their talk of ghosts and haunted houses, were, as Pope writes, like "The poor Indian whose untutored mind sees God in trees, hears him in the wind."

Jarvie Ricketts, somewhat of a mystic, a romancer, believed in the power of witchcraft. When a couple came to Netherstone, Polly Smith and her son Will, unusual things happened in the village under the Hill.

Fred Alderton's tale of Luke Coney had been simply for entertainment during an evening at the Cider Mill, but when things happened in the village Polly Smith was suspected of being a real witch. Will Smith worked on Park Farm. Jarvie said, "He had more than a touch of The Lawrence," meaning he was lazy.

Owen Pritchard was now running Park Farm for Tom Samson. He was a fair man, who expected a fair day's work from his men. Will Smith had been so slow hoeing swedes on a six acre field on the Hill that Owen's patience failed him and he beat young Will with his broad leather belt. At that time a hare leapt out and crossed his path. Nothing unusual in that, but even Owen believed that a boy at the local school suffered with a hare lip because his mother had walked close to a hare when she was expecting the child.

The morning after Owen had thrashed Will Smith, the horses in the stable were useless, worn out, unable to work. The cowman said they were hag rid. Polly shouted to Owen, "You beat my son. I'll wear out your horses."

Jarvie said that he had known horses come to the stable all of a muck sweat in the morning from the field, and this was known as hag ridden by witches.

"What shall we do?" Owen asked Jarvie.

"Hang a wreath of bryony over the stable door upside down." And, according to Jarvie, it worked.

"I wish she had never come to this Parish," Jack Lampit said as he supped his pint in the Cider Mill.

"She will have to be respected," Jarvie replied. "Nothing happens here without her knowing. She is bent and ugly, but that's not all."

"What else, Jarvie?" Jack asked, a tremble in his voice.

"She reads her Bible backwards to her black cat."

"That mead she makes from the honey bees in the garden is spiked with something very potent and gives folks who drink it a sense of flying, delirium. Some says 'tis Bella Donna."

"The girls in the village do walk miles when they go courting to avoid meeting her and her stare. They are convinced that Polly can read their thoughts and minds."

"'Tis like this," Jarvie continued, "I alluss keeps a few fags in my pocket 'cos if you don't give her something when you meet her she will cast a spell, and like enough the bacon will go bad on the flitch."

Polly the witch certainly had an effect on the simple folk of Netherstone. Both Ada Ricketts and Queenie

White were scared of her. They went for advice to Ruth Fairfax.

"Now look here, you have lived in Netherstone long enough to know that witchcraft will never harm you. Like nature we are dealing with the unexplained. Have you thought how wonderful God's world is? I have seen on Father's land wheat sown in November and harvested the following August. Isn't that like a child in the womb waiting nine months to be born?"

"Never thought of that," Queenie said with a sigh. "Nine months!"

"Oh, the cycle of the seasons intrigues me, but when James Bullen used to undersow the corn in spring with clover, that was not harvested until the following year, giving two cuts of clover hay, one in June, another in late July.

"What then?" Ruth continued with a twinkle in her eye, a young woman who knew the land they lived on. "In the autumn the aftermath clover, known here as the lattermath, is ploughed in, the fertility maintained for the crop, maybe field beans. This is what some call the rhythm of the season, sun, frost, rain, snow. Every April the cuckoo comes, the swallows pay a summer visit. They fly south only to be replaced by redwings or felts. They winter on the hedgerow, on crab apples, and leave again in the spring."

"Thank you, Ma,am," Ada said with some feeling. "You have put our minds at rest."

Ruth was pleased that she had been able to talk to the old women and said, "Now, don't you fret about Polly. She is not like us, I know. Her late husband, Wisdom

Smith, was somewhat of a mystic — they were travelling folk — but you needn't fear her."

For the villagers of Netherstone, all the old beliefs were strictly kept, whether they came from the Church or had originated in the days of their forefathers. Religion stood alongside folklore, and both played a part in the lives of these simple countryfolk.

Revd Mellor was in the custom of telling young mothers not to enter their neighbour's house until they had been churched. The churching of women was a part of the Prayer Book.

Other traditions were based on old sayings. "A whistling woman and a crowing hen are neither good for God nor men" — well, hens that crowed were soon dispatched and whistling women were warned.

Sometimes, seed corn was dressed in the barn with vitriol for smut and left in a heap on the barn floor. The sign of the Cross was roughly made with the shovel after the grain had been turned for the last time, another custom the villagers upheld.

No one ever burnt elder wood on the fire. It was always believed that it was an invitation for the Devil to come down the chimney.

Pigs were killed at the waxing of the moon for if the moon was on the wain the bacon would fry away in the pan.

Despite their worries about Polly, and their sometimes strange traditions and beliefs, the folk of Netherstone and the neighbouring villages got on with their life on the Hill. Some things would always remain unexplained to them, but surely there are mysteries in everything?

CHAPTER
TWENTY-FOUR

The Wartime Village

The Bullen brothers had been so much a part of Netherstone and Bredon Hill that their spirits, if not their faces, seemed ever-present around Cobblers Quar. Alf, the shepherd, folding the long-woolled Cotswold sheep on turnips, James, the carter, ploughing the limestone land with his old horses. When they had gone, men like Jarvie Ricketts, Jack Lampit and his "partner" Queenie kept up the old beliefs, the lore of the Hill, its secrets. They fended off the witch Polly Smith by giving her favours. They were afraid of her and found it better not to cross her. Who knows what evil she could cast in her spells?

Life continued for Henry Fairfax, released from his army service to manage the farm, taking the place of his father-in-law, Tom Samson. This was a community of simple folk with simple tackle, gathering the crops, tending the stock, with Owen Pritchard as Henry's right-hand man at Park Farm.

As was the nature of things in the countryside, younger men would take over from the aging farm labourers when they became too old to work the land. But when the Great War came, the young men were required to enlist.

Gerald Anderton joined the RAVC, his father's old regiment. Henry Fairfax, who had been Master of the Foxhounds, joined the Yeomanry. Daisy Sands's wayward son became a Conscientious Objector. He told Revd Mellor of his feelings about the war.

Henry Fairfax asked young Gerald one day, "What are you doing in the ranks, Alderton? You and your father have hunted the fox so many times. You take orders from me. I'm commissioning you on the battlefield as an Officer, and you will serve under me in the Gloucestershire Yoemanry."

When some of Henry Fairfax's young farm workers were called up, other older men stepped into their shoes on the Estate. Fred Chandler came as cowman while Walt from a neighbouring farm was carter. Alf Marsh had been shepherd for a Duke, but he settled with the hill flock of Kerry Hill ewes. Some of the much older villagers, through age, through the drama and stress of it all, seemed simply to fade away.

Fred Alderton, who had soldiered in the Boer War, was too old for service in 1914, but was an able Bailiff while Henry Fairfax had been away. (Because of the harvest Henry had leave from the army to bring in the crops at Park Farm and Sheldon.)

Sam, another veteran of South Africa, helped on the farms, working his smallholding part-time. His son was killed in France.

Charlie, the eldest son of a widow, was a smart soldier in the Worcestershire Regiment. His stories, when on leave, smacked of the brutality of war, the sacrifice of men's lives. Charlie told of one Officer in the

Worcesters who, after a ration of rum, had left the trench with bayonet fixed calling, "Come on Worcesters. The Hun are a hundred yards away." That brilliant young Officer was mortally wounded.

Young Charlie was affected by some of the things that happened to him, things he would never have dreamed of. He met a Prussian Guard who, at close range, aimed at Charlie. Perhaps it was this young Worcester's experience with a twelve-bore shooting rabbits, but it was the Prussian Guard who fell to Charlie's bullet, a wasted life. The young Worcester said, "When I saw the blood flow from his ears, caused by my bullet to his head, I cried, 'Oh My God, what have I done?'."

One of Charlie's village friends in the Worcesters, Sid, got married on leave, and then overstayed his leave. On returning to his Regiment, he was given Number One Field Punishment, as the Worcesters fought on the battlefield on the Western Front. In this case Sid was tied to the wheel of a gun carriage, his arms and legs outstretched. As the Germans advanced, the Worcesters retreated to positions behind the lines. Sid was shot with the machine guns. The news to his young widow said, "Killed in action." Charlie kept the truth to himself.

The New Year dawned in 1917 while many of the young men were in the mud of Flanders. Ruth Fairfax made sure some of the old customs remained. She invited Evan Pritchard from Park Farm to be first through her front door on New Year's Day, a tall dark man who came to wish the family luck and partake with the other bell-ringers of her cake and wine.

By the time Candlemas Fair came to Evesholme many of the best cart horses had been acquired by the military and Walt, the carter, was left with Duke, with a big knee, Captain, with a ridge back, and a couple of broken-winded old mares.

Alf Marsh's grandson, Geoff, lived at Lilac Cottage with the old couple. His father was serving in France, in what Alf called The Flying Corpse. Geoff had left school at thirteen and worked as plough boy on a neighbouring farm. This farmer sent him on a foolish errand on 1 April, All Fools Day. It seemed that this custom had always been observed on this farm. Geoff had to do as his master ordered. The farmer put stones and scrap iron into a sack, telling Geoff to take this to the next farm a mile away. He also gave him a note asking the neighbour for pigeon's milk, elbow grease and strap oil. At the first farm Geoff arrived at with his sack, the farmer looked at the note and said, "It's not for me, Boy. It's for George in the next village."

Away went Geoff loaded with trash, and George sent him on to the next village. This went on all morning until one kindly farmer told Geoff that his employer was trying to make him an April Fool, but now that twelve o'clock had past the employer was the biggest fool in the end.

Geoff returned with an empty sack but dare not tell his employer what the neighbour had said.

Tea-time at Lilac Cottage, and old Alf laughed over his mug of tea as he sat by the fire. "You can tell a cuckoo a mile away," the old man said. "And the cuckoo is your boss, but don't tell him so."

Jane Marsh baked some hot-cross buns for the family on Good Friday. "They must be cooked on Good Friday," she insisted as she put two or three in the ingle nook on a shelf by a side of bacon to keep for a year.

"Good for a young un with the belly-ache," Alf said with a chuckle. A cocoa can with acorns was among the remedies on that shelf too. "'Tis good for diarrhoea," the old man said, "and that brimstone your Grandma's gwain to give thee some with treacle. Spring medicine." The old man even looked after his sheep with ancient medicines and kept himself fit with agrimony tea.

May Day came but after the celebrations the Maypole in the village square was kept for the children to celebrate the Restoration of Charles II, Oak Apple Day, on 29 May.

Alf Marsh always read the local journal every Friday. As haymaking time came along, Sam Bennet, a Warwickshire morris dancer, put a piece in the paper that he had mowed an acre of grass with his scythe in an orchard.

"The old liar," Alf said as the smoke from his shag tobacco wafted in the chimney corner. "You see," he declared, "I've mowed an acre of grass, but in an orchard where you have to go around the apple trees, that's hindering. I knowed old Sam when I worked for the Duke, and Jimmy Teapot who kept the birds off the cherries, two of a kind mind."

Jane, who was a quiet little woman, said, "Alf, you know Sam could play that fiddle made in 1640 they say. Three hundred tunes he knew. They say he can play without music. Some of it has never been in print."

170

"Oh, I know old Sam in his Shakespearean smock and his morris dancing. He plays the fiddle, some other chap acts the fool with a pig's bladder on the end of a stick." Alf puffed hard on his clay pipe and added, "I've not much time myself for those acting-like hobbledehoys."

Shepherd Marsh came to Netherstone as a middle-aged man. He had worked on the Estate, near Evesholme, of the Duke of Orleans. The stories of Revd George Mellor and Benedict's Pool still remained as a vivid memory among the folk on Bredon Hill, but Alf Marsh treated such happenings with his usual cynicism. "I've lived too long in the woods to be frightened by owls," was a favourite saying of this shepherd.

Young Geoff Marsh, who had recently left school, worked on a neighbouring farm around the Hill. He drove the plough team for the carter there. It was quite usual for horses to be taken to Tom Atkins, the blacksmith, at a hamlet under the Hill to be shod. On wet days old Tom would have a number of horses there waiting their turn. On just such a day in December young Geoff took one of his master's horses there. He waited in the blacksmith's shop as the daylight faded, until at last Tom Atkins gave him a leg up onto one of the great black horses of the Midlands.

Geoff was not usually afraid of the dark but the way home from the smithy was past a quarry where a month before a man had been killed. Geoff had seen his body taken away from under a fall of stone. The memory stayed with him. Folk said that the man's ghost would be there for ever. This night was the first time that Geoff has passed the quarry in the dark. The rain abated, and a full moon rose over the Cotswolds, casting shadows from the naked roadside beech trees. All was quiet, men were at their firesides.

As Geoff approached the quarry he had a temptation to cast his eyes towards the spot, a ledge of rock, where the quarry man was killed. And there, a white figure stood with arms outstretched on that ledge. The boy's body froze and only slowly did life return to his young legs enabling him to give the mare the message to canter towards the farm. Then came the cry that his grandfather had called "the Hounds of Hell pursuing souls to Hades". No hound was seen but nonetheless Geoff arrived home in an agitated state.

"But Grandad," he said, "'Twas awful. The white creature on the ledge waving his arms and then the sound of that Hound of Hell."

"A drop of beetroot wine for you, Lad, and be soon to bed." His grannie tucked him well in that night, leaving the candle burning by the bedside. The couple talked of ghosts and the Hell Hounds and Jane was afraid of what Geoff had seen and heard.

Sep Sands, who lived near the quarry, kept poultry on his mother's small farm. As Christmas approached Sep's geese were fattening in the nag stable, but the old gander and some of the older birds still took a path past the quarry to Tom Samson's stubble fields, gleaning or, as was said locally, leasing. That evening as the moon was full the birds came late home. The old gander flew up onto the ledge of the quarry flapping his wings. Those old birds were able to take care of themselves from the foxes on the Hill. Renard, however, had killed some of

Sep's laying hens that he kept in a pen on the Hill. Sep had a big Scottish collie named Brock, so-called because of his badger-like face. Brock was kept chained up by the fowl pen to guard the hens from Renard.

The evening when Geoff Marsh returned from the smithy was the evening of the full moon. It's strange how dogs do bay at the moon with a particular howl, a blood-curdling noise in the still of the night. The Hound of Hell on Bredon that December night was none other than Brock baying at the full moon and the ghost was Sep's gander roosting on the ledge of the quarry.

So after all, Geoff had been quite safe, and his grandad and grandma continued to look after him during those long war-time years.

CHAPTER
TWENTY-FIVE

From Horse Power to Tractor Power

After 1918, when the war ended, men could be seen around Netherstone clad in army clothes: heavy coats, tunics, some sported the breeches of men who had served in the Horse Artillery. Khaki puttees were favoured by the men on the land; they were warm and kept their legs dry in those pre-Wellington days.

Like so many towns and villages, Netherstone had suffered the loss of its young men. Those who followed were of a different ilk, with fancy clothes and bicycles to go to the cinemas on Saturday nights. And there were other changes on the land too.

Like the old men of the village, the horses were growing slower as the years passed, and in 1917 Henry Ford sent over from the United States the first of his tractors. The iron-cleated wheels marked the land where, for centuries, the horses had ploughed, sowed and reaped. As the Fordson first came to Netherstone to mow the hayfields, taking the place of the staid and trusty Shire horses, Shepherd Marsh voiced his opinion. Picking up a wisp of hay he sniffed it. "Stinks of paraffin," he said. "My ewes won't eat this tack."

Gilbert, from the iron seat of the Fordson, replied, "The horses are old, Shepherd. I can't find two who will pull the mower."

"'Tis very bad to see my 'osses that have worked for twenty years going to the knackers." Walt, with raised eyebrows, couldn't see what else could be done but for Gilbert to till the soil and cut the hay using a tractor.

It seemed that in those early years after the war the men who had worked the land just faded away. Some, like Walt, stayed with the remnants of his former team of horses, foddering with a cart on winter days, doing odd jobs around the farm. Henry Fairfax, as the new farmer, took no delight in seeing old men go from the land, and old horses too. The Pritchards were his main workmen. Gilbert Pritchard made an expert ploughman with his tractor. It was said in those early days of mechanisation that to teach a horse ploughman to plough with a tractor proved better than teaching a tractor driver to plough with a horse.

Netherstone and Walt, now retired, looked back at the Bullens who tilled the land, shepherded the sheep. The horses went one at a time, replaced by the tractor and Gilbert. And the men, too, slowly disappeared. Revd George Mellor laid so many of his flock to rest in the Churchyard.

Ruth, who had been such a stalwart for the Church and the land at Netherstone, now a wife to Henry Fairfax, viewed the changes philosophically. She impressed on her husband that she accepted the inevitable. And she had understood how the Bullen brothers had been bewitched by real fears of evil spirits. She had calmed those fears when she explained how they were unfounded.

Walt and Captain, the last of the horse teams, remained until Captain died. The tractor did give the scent of paraffin to the hay, just as Shepherd Marsh had said, but even so it was the first machine of thousands to follow.

As the tractors came and the old farming ways died, it seemed like a bit of the real Netherstone died too. The Bullens, Jarvie Ricketts, Jack Ford, Sep Sands, Joe Badger — all of these were no more. But their spirits live on in the hills around Netherstone, and when the wind whispers over the waters of Benedict's Pool perhaps mixed in with it one can hear them gossiping still around a table at the old Cider Mill.

ISIS publish a wide range of books in large print, from fiction to biography. A full list of titles is available free of charge from the address below. Alternatively, contact your local library for details of their collection of ISIS large print books.

Details of ISIS complete and unabridged audio books are also available.

Any suggestions for books you would like to see in large print or audio are always welcome.

7 Centremead
Osney Mead
Oxford OX2 0ES
(01865) 250333